Absolute Surrender

Absolute Surrender

Andrew Murray

WHITAKER
HOUSE

Publisher's note:
This new edition from Whitaker House has been updated for the
modern reader. Words, expressions, and sentence structure have
been revised for clarity and readability.

All Scripture quotations are taken from the
King James Version of the Holy Bible.

ABSOLUTE SURRENDER

ISBN: 978-0-88368-093-3
eBook ISBN: 978-1-60374-423-2
Printed in the United States of America
© 1981, 2013 by Whitaker House

Whitaker House
1030 Hunt Valley Circle
New Kensington, PA 15068
www.whitakerhouse.com

20 21 22 23 24 25 26   **ω**   23 22 21 20 19 18 17

CONTENTS

1

ABSOLUTE SURRENDER

Now Ben-Hadad the king of Syria gathered all his forces together; thirty-two kings were with him, with horses and chariots. And he went up and besieged Samaria, and made war against it. Then he sent messengers into the city to Ahab king of Israel, and said to him, "Thus says Ben-Hadad: 'Your silver and your gold are mine; your loveliest wives and children are mine.'" And the king of Israel answered and said, "My lord, O king, just as you say, I and all that I have are yours."
—1 Kings 20:1–4

Ahab gave what was asked of him by Ben-hadad—absolute surrender. I want to use these words, "My lord, O king, just as you say, I and all that I have are yours," as the words of absolute surrender with which every child

7

of God ought to yield himself to his Father. We have heard it before, but we need to hear it very definitely— the condition of God's blessing is absolute surrender of everything into His hands. Praise God! If our hearts are willing for this, there is no end to what God will do for us, and to the blessing God will bestow.

Absolute surrender—let me tell you where I got those words. I used them myself often, and you have heard them numerous times. But once, in Scotland, I was part of a group of people talking about the condition of Christ's church, and what the great need of the church and of believers is. There was in our group a godly Christian worker who was involved in training other workers for Christ, and I asked him what he would say was the great need of the church—the message that ought to be preached. He answered very quietly and simply and determinedly, "Absolute surrender to God is the one thing."

The words struck me as never before. And that man began to tell how, in the Christian workers whom he trained, he found that if they were sound on that point, they were willing to be taught and helped, and they always improved. Conversely, others who were not sound there very often went back and left the work. The condition for obtaining God's full blessing is *absolute surrender* to Him.

And now, I desire by God's grace to give to you this message—that your God in heaven answers the prayers that you have offered for blessing on yourselves and for blessing on those around you by this one demand: *Are you willing to surrender yourselves absolutely into His hands?* What is our answer to be? God knows there are hundreds of hearts who have said it, and there are hundreds more who long to say it but hardly dare to do so. And there are hearts who have said it, yet who have miserably failed, and who feel themselves condemned because they did not find the secret of the power to live that life. May God have a word for all!

Let me say, first of all, that God expects it from us.

God Expects Your Surrender

Yes, absolute surrender has its foundation in the very nature of God. God cannot do otherwise. Who is God? He is the Fountain of life, the only Source of existence and power and goodness. Throughout the universe there is nothing good but what God works. God has created the sun, the moon, the stars, the flowers, the trees, and the grass. Are they not all absolutely surrendered to God? Do they not allow God to work in them just what He pleases? When God clothes the lily with its beauty, is it not yielded up, surrendered, given over to God as He works in it its beauty? (See Matthew 6:28–29.) And God's redeemed children— can you think that God can do His work if there is only half or a part of them surrendered? God cannot do it. God is life, love, blessing, power, and infinite beauty, and God delights in communicating Himself to every child who is prepared to receive Him. But this lack of absolute surrender is just the thing that hinders God. And now He comes, and as God, He claims it.

You know in daily life what absolute surrender is. You know that everything has to be given up to its special, definite purpose and service. I have a pen in my pocket, and that pen is absolutely surrendered to the one work of writing. That pen must be absolutely surrendered to my hand if I am to write properly with it. If another person holds it partly, I cannot write properly. This coat I am wearing is absolutely given up to me to cover my body. This building is entirely given up to religious services. And now, do you expect that in your immortal being, in the divine nature that you have received by regeneration, God can work His work, every day and every hour, unless you are entirely given up to Him? God cannot. The temple of Solomon was absolutely surrendered to God when it was dedicated to Him. And every one of us is a temple of God, in which God will dwell and work mightily on one condition—absolute surrender to Him. God claims it, God is worthy of it, and without it God cannot work His blessed work in us.

God not only claims it, but God will work it Himself.

God Accomplishes Your Surrender

I am sure there are many hearts that say, "Ah, but that absolute surrender implies so much!" Someone says, "Oh, I have passed through so much trial and suffering, and there is so much of the self-life still remaining. I dare not face entirely giving it up because I know it will cause so much trouble and agony."

Alas! How unfortunate that God's children have such thoughts of Him, such cruel thoughts. I come with a message to those who are fearful and anxious. God does not ask you to give the perfect surrender in your strength, or by the power of your will; God is willing to work it in you. Do we not read, *"It is God who works in you both to will and to do for His good pleasure"* (Philippians 2:13)? And that is what we should seek—to go on our faces before God, until our hearts learn to believe that the everlasting God Himself will come in to drive out what is wrong. He will conquer what is evil and work what is well-pleasing in His blessed sight. God Himself will work it in you.

Look at the men in the Old Testament, like Abraham. Do you think it was by accident that God found that man, the father of the faithful and the friend of God? Do you think it was Abraham himself, apart from God, who had such faith and such obedience and such devotion? You know it is not so. God raised him up and prepared him as an instrument for His glory.

Did God not say to Pharaoh, *"For this purpose I have raised you up, that I may show My power in you"* (Exodus 9:16)? And if God said that of him, will God not say it far more of every child of His?

Oh, I want to encourage you, and I want you to cast away every fear. Come with that feeble desire. If there is the fear that says, "Oh, my desire is not strong enough. I am not willing to accept everything that may come, and I do not feel bold enough to say I can conquer everything," then I implore you, learn to know and trust your God now. Say to Him, "My God, I am willing that You should make me willing." If there is anything holding you back, or any sacrifice you are afraid of making, come to God now and prove how gracious your God is. Do not be afraid that He will command from you what He will not bestow.

God comes and offers to work this absolute surrender in you. All these searchings and hungerings and longings that are in your heart, I tell you, they are the drawings of the divine magnet, Christ Jesus. He lived a life of absolute surrender. He has possession of you; He is living in your heart by His Holy Spirit. You have hindered Him terribly, but He desires to help you to get a hold of Him entirely. And He comes and draws you now by His message and words. Will you not come and trust God to work in you that absolute surrender to Himself? Yes, blessed be God! He can do it, and He will do it.

God not only claims it and works it, but God accepts it when we bring it to Him.

God Accepts Your Surrender

God works it in the secret places of our hearts; God urges us by the hidden power of His Holy Spirit to come and speak it out, and we have to bring and yield to Him that absolute surrender. But remember, when you come and bring God that absolute surrender, it may, as far as your feelings or your consciousness goes, be a thing of great imperfection. You may doubt and hesitate and say, "Is it absolute?"

But remember, there was once a man to whom Christ had said, *"If you can believe, all things are possible to him who believes"* (Mark 9:23). And his heart was afraid, and he cried out, *"Lord, I believe; help my unbelief!"* (verse 24).

That was a faith that triumphed over Satan, and the evil spirit was cast out. And if you come and say, "Lord, I yield myself in absolute surrender to my God," even though you do so with a trembling heart and with the consciousness, "I do not feel the power; I do not feel the determination; I do not feel the assurance," it will succeed. Do not be afraid, but come just as you are. Even in the midst of your trembling, the power of the Holy Spirit will work.

Have you not yet learned the lesson that the Holy Spirit works with mighty power, while on the human side everything appears feeble? Look at the Lord Jesus Christ in Gethsemane. We read that He, *"through the eternal Spirit"* (Hebrews 9:14), offered Himself as a sacrifice unto God. The almighty Spirit of God was enabling Him to do it. And yet, what agony and fear and exceeding sorrow came over Him, and how He prayed! Externally, you can see no sign of the mighty power of the Spirit, but the Spirit of God was there. And even so, while you are feeble and fighting and trembling, with faith in the hidden work of God's Spirit do not fear, but yield yourself.

And when you do yield yourself in absolute surrender, let it be with the faith that God does now accept it. This is the great point, and this is what we so often miss—that believers should be thus occupied with God in this matter of surrender. Be occupied with God. We need to get help, every one of us, so that in our daily lives God will be clearer to us, God will have the right place, and be all in all. And if we are to have this through life, let us begin now and look away from ourselves and look up to God. Let each one believe, "I, a poor worm on earth and a trembling child of God, full of failure, sin, and fear, bow here, and no one knows what passes through my heart." Simply say, "Oh God, I accept Your terms. I have pleaded for blessing on myself and others. I have accepted Your terms of absolute surrender." While your heart says this in deep silence, remember there is a God present who takes note of it and writes it down in His book. There is a God present who at that very moment takes possession of you. You may not feel it, you may not realize it, but God takes possession if you will trust Him.

God not only claims it and works it and accepts it when I bring it, but God also maintains it.

God Maintains Your Surrender

This is the great difficulty with many. People say, "I have often been stirred at a meeting or at a convention, and I have consecrated myself to God. But it has passed away. I know it may last for a week or for a month, but it fades away. After a time it is all gone."

But listen! It is because you do not believe what I am now going to tell you and remind you of. When God has begun the work of absolute surrender in you, and when God has accepted your surrender, then God holds Himself bound to care for it and to keep it. Will you believe that?

In this matter of surrender, there are two participants: God and you—God the everlasting and omnipotent Jehovah, and you a worm. (See Job 25:6.) Worm, will you be afraid to trust yourself to this mighty God now? God is willing. Do you not believe that He can keep you continually, day by day, and moment by moment?

Moment by moment I'm kept in His love;
Moment by moment I've life from above.

If God allows the sun to shine on you moment by moment, without intermission, will God not let His life shine on you every moment? And why have you not experienced it? Because you have not trusted God for it, and you do not surrender yourself absolutely to God in that trust.

A life of absolute surrender has its difficulties. I do not deny that. Yes, it has something far more than difficulties; it is a life that is absolutely impossible by man's own power. But by the grace of God, by the power of God, by the power of the Holy Spirit dwelling in us, it is a life to which we are destined, and a life that is possible for us. Praise God! Let us believe that God will maintain it.

Some of you have read the words of George Müller, who, on his ninetieth birthday, told of all God's goodness to him. What did he say he believed to be the secret of his happiness and of all the blessing that God had given him? He said he believed there were two reasons. The one was that he had been enabled by grace to maintain a good conscience before God day by day. The other was that he was a lover of God's Word. Ah, yes, a good conscience is complete obedience to God day by day, and fellowship with God every day in His Word and prayer—that is a life of absolute surrender.

Such a life has two sides. On one side, there is absolute surrender to work what God wants you to do; on the other side, you must let God work what *He* wants to do.

First, what does it mean to do what God wants you to do?

Give yourselves up absolutely to the will of God. You know something of that will; not enough, far from all. But say absolutely to the Lord God, "By Your grace I desire to do Your will in everything, every moment of every day." Say, "Lord God, not a word upon my tongue but for Your glory. Not a movement of my temper but for Your glory. Not a feeling of love or hate in my heart but for Your glory, and according to Your blessed will."

Someone says, "Do you think that is possible?"

I ask, What has God promised you, and what can God do to fill a vessel absolutely surrendered to Him? Oh, God wants to bless you in a way beyond what you expect. From the beginning, no ear has heard, no eye has seen what God has prepared for those who love Him. (See 1 Corinthians 2:9.) God has prepared unheard-of things, blessings much more wonderful than you can imagine, more mighty than you can picture. They are divine blessings. Oh, say now, "I give myself absolutely to God, to His will, to do only what God wants."

It is God who will enable you to carry out the surrender.

And, on the other side, come and say, "I give myself absolutely to God, to let Him work in me 'to will *and to do for His good pleasure'* (Philippians 2:13), as He has promised to do."

Yes, the living God wants to work in His children in a way that we cannot understand, but that God's Word has revealed. He wants to work in us every moment of the day. God is willing to maintain our lives. Only let our absolute surrender be one of simple, childlike, and unbounded trust.

God Blesses When You Surrender

This absolute surrender to God brings wonderful blessings.

What Ahab said to his enemy, King Ben-hadad, will we not say to our God and loving Father? *"My lord, O king, just as you say, I and all that I have are yours."* If we do say it, God's blessing will come upon us. God wants us to be separate from the world. We are called to come out from the world that hates God. Come out for God and say, "Lord, anything for You." If you say this with prayer and speak this into God's ear, He will accept it, and He will teach you what it means.

I say again, God will bless you. You have been praying for blessing. But do remember, there must be absolute surrender. Why is tea poured into a cup? Because it is empty, and given up to the tea. But put ink or vinegar or wine into it, and will anyone pour tea into the cup? Likewise, can God fill you, can God bless you if you are not absolutely surrendered to Him? He cannot. Let us believe that God has wonderful blessings for us if we will only stand up for God and say, though it may be with trembling wills, yet with believing hearts, "O God, I accept Your demands. I and all that I have are Yours. Absolute surrender is what my soul yields to You by divine grace."

You may not have such strong, clear feelings of surrender as you would like to have, but humble yourself in His sight, and acknowledge that you have grieved the Holy Spirit by your self-will, self-confidence, and self-effort. Bow humbly before Him, confessing your self-reliance, and ask Him to break your heart and to bring you into the dust before Him. Then, as you bow before Him, just accept God's teaching that in your flesh *"nothing good dwells"* (Romans 7:18), and that nothing will help you except another life that must come in. You must deny self once and for all. Denying self must every moment be the power of your life, and then Christ will come in and take possession of you.

When was Peter delivered? When was the change accomplished? The change began with Peter weeping, and the Holy Spirit came down and filled his heart.

God the Father loves to give us the power of the Spirit. We have the Spirit of God dwelling within us. We come to God confessing this, and praising God for it, and yet confessing how we have grieved the Spirit. And then we bow our knees to the Father to ask that He would strengthen us with all might by the Spirit in the inner man, and that He would fill us with His mighty power. (See Ephesians 3:14–19.) And as the Spirit reveals Christ to us, Christ comes to live in our hearts forever, and the self-life is cast out.

Let us bow before God in humility, and in that humility confess before Him the state of the whole church. No words can tell the sad state of the church of Christ on earth. I wish I had words to speak what I sometimes feel about it. Just think of the Christians around you. I do not speak of nominal Christians, or of professing Christians, but I speak of hundreds and thousands of honest, earnest Christians who are not living a life in the power of God or to His glory. So little power, so little devotion or consecration to God, so little perception of the truth that a Christian is a man utterly surrendered to God's will! Oh, we need to confess the sins of God's people around us and to humble ourselves.

We are members of that sickly body. The sickliness of the body will hinder us and break us down unless we come to God. We must, in confession, separate ourselves from partnership with worldliness, with coldness toward each other. We must give ourselves up to be entirely and wholly for God.

How much Christian work is being done in the spirit of the flesh and in the power of self! How much work goes on, day by day, in which human energy—our wills and our thoughts about the work—is continually manifested, and in which there is little waiting upon God and upon the power of the Holy Spirit! Let us make a confession. But as we confess the state of the church, and the feebleness and sinfulness of work for God among us, let us come back to ourselves. Who is there who truly longs to be delivered from the power of the self-life, who truly acknowledges that it is the power of self and the flesh, and who is willing to cast all at the feet of Christ? There is deliverance.

I heard of one who had been an earnest Christian, and who spoke about the "cruel" thought of separation and death. But you do not think that, do you? What are we to think of separation and death? We are to think that this death is the path to glory for Christ. Christ, *" for the joy that was set before Him*[,] *endured the cross"* (Hebrews 12:2). The Cross was the birthplace of His everlasting glory. Do you love Christ? Do you long to be in Christ, and yet not *like* Him? Let death be to you the most desirable thing on earth—death to self, and fellowship with Christ. Separation—do you think it a hard thing to be called to be entirely free from the world, and by that separation to be united to God and His love, by separation to become prepared for living and walking with God every day? Surely one ought to say, "Anything to bring me to separation, to death, for a life of full fellowship with God and Christ."

Come and cast this self-life and flesh-life at the feet of Jesus. Then trust Him. Do not worry yourselves with trying to understand everything about it, but come in the living faith that Christ will come into you with the power of His death and the power of His life. Then the Holy Spirit will bring the whole Christ—Christ crucified and risen and living in glory—into your hearts.

2

THE SPIRIT OF LOVE

The fruit of the Spirit is love.
—Galatians 5:22

I want to look at the life filled with the Holy Spirit more from the practical side. I want to show how this life will reveal itself in our daily walk and conduct.

Under the Old Testament, the Holy Spirit often came upon men as a divine Spirit of revelation to reveal the mysteries of God, or for power to do the work of God. But He did not dwell in them then. Now, many people want just the Old Testament gift of power for work, but they know very little of the New Testament gift of the indwelling Spirit, animating and renewing the whole life. When God gives the Holy Spirit, His great purpose is the formation of a holy character. It is a gift of a holy mind and spiritual disposition, and what we need, above everything else, is to say, "I must have the Holy Spirit sanctifying my whole inner life if I am really to live for God's glory."

You might say that when Christ promised the Spirit to the disciples, He did so in order that they might have power to be witnesses. True, but then they received the Holy Spirit in such heavenly power and reality that He took possession of their whole beings at once and equipped them as holy men for doing the work with power as they had to do it. Christ spoke of power to the disciples, but it was the Spirit filling their whole beings that worked the power.

I wish now to dwell upon the passage found in Galatians 5:22: "*The fruit of the Spirit is love.*"

We read that "*love is the fulfillment of the law*" (Romans 13:10), and my desire is to tell of love as a fruit of the Spirit with a twofold purpose. One is that this word may be a searchlight in our hearts, and give us a test by which to try all our thoughts about the Holy Spirit and all our experience of the holy life. Let us try ourselves by this word. Has this been our daily habit, to seek to be filled with the Holy Spirit as the

Spirit of love? *"The fruit of the Spirit is love."* Has it been our experience that the more we have of the Holy Spirit, the more loving we become? In claiming the Holy Spirit, we should make this the first object of our expectation. The Holy Spirit comes as a Spirit of love.

Oh, if this were true in the church of Christ, how different her state would be! May God help us to get hold of this simple, heavenly truth, that the fruit of the Spirit is a love that appears in the life. Just as the Holy Spirit gets real possession of the life, the heart will be filled with real, divine, universal love.

One of the great reasons why God cannot bless His church is the lack of love. When the body is divided, there cannot be strength. In the time of their great religious wars, when Holland stood out so nobly against Spain, one of their mottoes was, "Unity gives strength." Only when God's people stand as one body, one before God in the fellowship of love, one toward another in deep affection, one before the world in a love that the world can see—only then will they have power to secure the blessing that they ask of God.

Remember that if a vessel that ought to be whole is cracked into many pieces, it cannot be filled. You can take one part of the vessel and dip a little water into that, but if you want the vessel full, the vessel must be whole. This is literally true of Christ's church. And if there is one thing we must pray for still, it is this: "Lord, melt us together into one by the power of the Holy Spirit. Let the Holy Spirit, who at Pentecost made them all of one heart and one soul, do His blessed work among us." Praise God, we can love each other in a divine love, for *"the fruit of the Spirit is love."* Give yourselves up to love, and the Holy Spirit will come; receive the Spirit, and He will teach you to love more.

God Is Love

Now, why is it that the fruit of the Spirit is love? Because *"God is love"* (1 John 4:8).

And what does this mean?

It is the very nature and being of God to delight in communicating Himself. God has no selfishness; God keeps nothing to Himself. God's nature is to be always giving. You see it in the sun and the moon and the stars, in every flower, in every bird in the air, in every fish in the sea. God communicates life to His creatures. And the angels around His throne, the seraphim and cherubim who are flames of fire—where does their glory come from? It comes from God because He is love, and He imparts to them part of His brightness and His blessedness. And we, His redeemed children—God delights to pour His love into us. Why? Because, as I said, God keeps nothing for Himself. From eternity God had His only begotten Son, and the Father gave Him all things, and nothing that God had was kept back. *"God is love"* (1 John 4:8).

One of the old church fathers said that we cannot better understand the Trinity than as a revelation of divine love—the Father, the loving One, the Fountain of love; the Son, the beloved One, the Reservoir of love, in whom the love was poured out; and the Spirit, the living love that united both and then overflowed into this world. The Spirit of Pentecost, the Spirit of the Father, the Spirit of the Son is love. And when the Holy Spirit comes to us and to other men and women, will He be less a Spirit of love than He is in God? It cannot be; He cannot change His nature. The Spirit of God is love, and *"the fruit of the Spirit is love."*

Mankind Needs Love

Love was the one great need of mankind, the thing that Christ's redemption came to accomplish: to restore love to this world.

When man sinned, why did he sin? Selfishness triumphed; he sought self instead of God. And just look! Adam at once began to accuse the woman of having led him astray. Love of God had gone; love of man was lost. Also consider that, of Adam's first two children, the one became a murderer of his brother.

Does this not teach us that sin had robbed the world of love? Oh, what a proof the history of the world has been of love having been lost! There may have been beautiful examples of love even among the heathen, but only as a little remnant of what was lost. One of the worst things sin did for man was to make him selfish, for selfishness cannot love.

The Lord Jesus Christ came down from heaven as the Son of God's love. *"God so loved the world that He gave His only begotten Son"* (John 3:16). God's Son came to show what love is, and He lived a life of love here on earth in fellowship with His disciples, in compassion over the poor and miserable, in love even for His enemies. He died the death of love. When He went back to heaven, whom did He send down? The Spirit of love, to come and banish selfishness and envy and pride, and to bring the love of God into the hearts of men. *"The fruit of the Spirit is love."*

And what was the preparation for the promise of the Holy Spirit? Before Christ promised the Holy Spirit, He gave a new commandment, and about that new commandment He said wonderful things. One thing was, *"As I have loved you,...love one another"* (John 13:34). To them His dying love was to be the only law of their conduct and fellowship with each other. What a message to those fishermen, to those men full of pride and selfishness! "Learn to love each other," said Christ, "as I have loved you." And by the grace of God they did it. When Pentecost came, they *"were of one heart and one soul"* (Acts 4:32). Christ did it for them.

And now He calls us to live and to walk in love. He demands that, though a man hate you, still you must love him. (See Matthew 5:44.) True love cannot be conquered by anything in heaven or on earth. The more hatred there is, the more love triumphs through it all and shows its true nature. This is the love that Christ commanded His disciples to exercise.

What more did He say? *"By this all will know that you are My disciples, if you have love for one another"* (John 13:35).

You all know what it is to wear a badge. And Christ said to His disciples, in effect, "I give you a badge, and that badge is love. That is to be your mark. It is the only thing in heaven or on earth by which men can know Me."

Do we not begin to fear that love has fled from the earth? That if we were to ask the world, "Have you seen us wear the badge of love?" the world would say, "No, what we have heard of the church of Christ is that there is not a place where there is no quarreling and separation"? Let us ask God with one heart that we may wear the badge of Jesus' love. God is able to give it.

Love Conquers Selfishness

"The fruit of the Spirit is love." Why? Because nothing but love can expel and conquer our selfishness.

Self is the great curse, whether in its relation to God, to our fellowmen in general, or to fellow

Christians. It causes us to think of ourselves and to seek our own way. Self is our greatest curse. But, praise God, Christ came to redeem us from self. We sometimes talk about deliverance from the self-life— and thank God for every word that can be said about it to help us. But I am afraid some people think deliverance from the self-life means that now they are no longer going to have any trouble in serving God. They forget that deliverance from self-life means to be a vessel overflowing with love to everybody all day long.

And here you have the reason why many people pray for the power of the Holy Spirit. They get something, but oh, so little, because they prayed for power for work, and power for blessing, but they have not prayed for power for full deliverance from self. This means not only the righteous self in fellowship with God, but also the unloving self in fellowship with men. And there is deliverance. "*The fruit of the Spirit is love.*" I bring you the glorious promise of Christ that He is able to fill our hearts with love.

A great many of us try hard at times to love. We try to force ourselves to love, and I do not say this is wrong; it is better than nothing. But the end of it is always very sad. "I fail continually," many must confess. And what is the reason? The reason is simply this: they have never learned to believe and accept the truth that the Holy Spirit can pour God's love into their heart. The blessed Scripture has often been limited—"*The love of God has been poured out in our hearts*" (Romans 5:5). It has often been understood only in the sense that the love of God has been poured out *to me*. Oh, what a limitation! That is only the beginning. The love of God is always the love of God in its entirety, in its fullness as an indwelling power. It is a love of God for me that leaps back to Him in love, and overflows to my fellowmen in love—God's love for me, and my love for God, and my love for my fellowmen. The three are one; you cannot separate them.

Believe that the love of God can be poured out in your heart and mind so that you can love throughout the day.

"Oh," you say, "how little I have understood that!"

Why is a lamb always gentle? Because that is its nature. Does it cost the lamb any trouble to be gentle? No. Why not? It is so beautiful and gentle. Must a lamb study to be gentle? No. Why does it come so easily? It is its nature. And a wolf—why does it cost a wolf no trouble to be cruel, and to put its fangs into the poor lamb or sheep? Because that is its nature. It does not have to summon up its courage; the wolf's nature is there.

And how can I learn to love? I cannot learn to love until the Spirit of God fills my heart with God's love, and I begin to long for God's love in a very different sense from which I have sought it so selfishly—as a comfort, a joy, a happiness, and a pleasure to myself. I will not learn it until I realize that *"God is love"* (1 John 4:8), and I claim and receive it as an indwelling power for self-sacrifice. I will not love until I begin to see that my glory, my blessedness, is to be like God and like Christ, in giving up everything in myself for my fellowmen. May God teach us this! Oh, the divine blessedness of the love with which the Holy Spirit can fill our hearts! *"The fruit of the Spirit is love."*

Love Is God's Gift

Why do we need God to give us love? My answer is, Without His love we cannot live the daily life of love.

How often, when we speak about the conse-crated life, we have to speak about *temperament*, and people have sometimes said, "You make too much of temperament."

I do not think we can make too much of it. Think for a moment of a clock and of what its hands mean. The hands tell me what is within the clock, and if I see that the hands stand still, or that the hands point wrong, or that the clock is slow or fast, I say that something inside the clock is not working properly. A person's temperament is just like the revelation that the clock's face gives of what is within. Temperament is proof of whether the love of Christ is filling the heart or not. There are many people who find it easier in church, in prayer meeting, or in work for the Lord— diligent, earnest work—to be holy and happy than in their daily lives with their families. How many find it easier to be holy and happy outside the home than in it! Where is the love of God? In Christ. God has prepared for us a wonderful redemption in Christ, and He longs to make something supernatural of us. Have we learned to long for it, ask for it, and expect it in its fullness?

Then there is the tongue! We sometimes speak of the tongue when we talk of the better life and the restful life, but just think what liberty many Christians give to their tongues. They say, "I have a right to say what I please."

When they speak about each other, when they speak about their neighbors, when they speak about other Christians, how often there are sharp remarks! May God keep me from saying anything that would be unloving. May God shut my mouth if I am not speaking in tender love. What I am saying is a fact. How often sharp criticism, harsh judgment, hasty opinion, unloving words, secret contempt and condemnation of each other are found among Christians who are banded together in work! Oh, just as a mother's love covers her children, delights in them, and has the tenderest compassion with their foibles or failures, so there ought to be in the heart of every believer a motherly love toward every brother and sister in Christ. Have you aimed at that? Have you sought it? Have you ever pleaded for it? Jesus Christ said, *"As I have loved you,…love one another"* (John 13:34). And He did not put that among the other commandments, but He said, in effect, "This is a new commandment, the one commandment: Love one another as I have loved you."

It is in our daily lives and conduct that *"the fruit of the Spirit is love."* From this source come all the graces and virtues in which love is manifested—joy, peace, long-suffering, gentleness, goodness, no sharpness or hardness in your tone, no unkindness or selfishness, meekness before God and man. You see that all these are the gentler virtues. I have often thought as I read those words in Colossians, *"Therefore, as the elect of God, holy and beloved, put on tender mercies, kindness, humility, meekness, longsuffering"* (Colossians 3:12), that if we had written this, we would have put in the foreground the strong virtues, such as zeal, courage, and diligence. But we need to see how the gentler, the tenderest virtues are especially connected with dependence on the Holy Spirit. These are indeed heavenly graces. They never were found in the heathen world. Christ was needed to come from heaven to teach us. Your blessedness is long-suffering, meekness, kindness; your glory is humility before God. The fruit of the Spirit that He brought from heaven out of the heart of the crucified Christ, and that He gives in our hearts, is, first and foremost, love.

You know what John said: *"No one has seen God at any time. If we love one another, God abides in us"* (1 John 4:12). That is, I cannot see God, but as compensation, I can see my brother, and if I love him, God dwells in me. Is that really true—that I cannot see God, but I must love my brother, and God will dwell in me? Loving my brother is the way to real fellowship with God. You know what John further said in that most solemn test: *"If someone says, 'I love God,' and hates his brother, he is a liar; for he who does not love his brother whom he has seen, how can he love God whom he has not seen?"* (1 John 4:20).

You might know of someone who is most unlovable. He upsets you every time you meet him. His disposition is the very opposite to yours. You are a careful businessman, and you have to associate with him in your business. He is untidy, unbusinesslike. You say, "I cannot love him." Oh, friend, you have not learned the lesson that Christ wanted to teach above everything. Let a man be what he will; you are to love him. Love is to be the fruit of the Spirit all day long and every day. Yes, listen! If you don't love that unlovable man whom you have seen, how can you love God whom you have not seen? You can deceive yourself with beautiful thoughts about loving God. You must prove your love for God by your love for your brother; this is the one standard by which God will judge your love for Him. If the love of God is in your heart, you will love your brother. *"The fruit of the Spirit is love."*

And what is the reason why God's Holy Spirit cannot come in power? Is it not possible?

You remember the comparison I used in speaking of the vessel. I can put a little water into a small vessel, but if a vessel is to be full, it must be unbroken. And the children of God, wherever they come together, to whatever church or congregation they belong, must love each other intensely, or the Spirit of God cannot do His work. We talk about grieving the Spirit of God by worldliness and ritualism and formality and error and indifference. But I tell you, the one thing above everything that grieves God's Spirit is this lack of love. Let every heart search itself and ask that God may search it.

Our Love Shows God's Power

Why are we taught that *"the fruit of the Spirit is love"*? Because the Spirit of God has come to make our daily lives an exhibition of divine power and a revelation of what God can do for His children.

In Acts, we read that the disciples were *"of one heart and one soul"* (Acts 4:32). During the three years they had walked with Christ, they never had been in that spirit. All Christ's teaching could not make them *"of one heart and one soul."* But the Holy Spirit came from heaven and poured out the love of God in their hearts, and they were *"of one heart and one soul."* The same Holy Spirit that brought the love of heaven into their hearts must fill us, too. Nothing less will do. Even as Christ did, one might preach love for three years with the tongue of an angel (see 1 Corinthians 13:1), but that would not teach any man to love unless the power of the Holy Spirit came upon him to bring the love of heaven into his heart.

Think of the church at large. What divisions! Think of the different bodies. Take the question of holiness, take the question of the cleansing blood, take the question of the baptism of the Spirit—what differences are caused among believers by such questions! That there are differences of opinion does not trouble me. We do not all have the same temperament and mind. But how often hate, bitterness, contempt, separation, and unlovingness are caused by the holiest truths of God's Word! Our doctrines, our creeds, have been more important than love. We often think we are valiant for the truth, and we forget God's command to speak *"the truth in love"* (Ephesians 4:15). And it was so in the time of the Reformation between the Lutheran and Calvinistic churches. What bitterness there was in regard to Communion, which was meant to be the bond of union among all believers! And so, through the ages, the very dearest truths of God have become mountains that have separated us.

If we want to pray in power, if we want to expect the Holy Spirit to come down in power, and if we indeed want God to pour out His Spirit, we must enter into a covenant with God that we will love one another with a heavenly love.

Are you ready for this? Only this is true love that is large enough to take in all God's children, the most unloving and unlovable and unworthy and unbearable and trying. If my vow—absolute surrender to God—is sincere, then it must mean absolute surrender to the divine love to fill me. I must be a servant of love to love every child of God around me. *"The fruit of the Spirit is love."*

Oh, God did something wonderful when He gave Christ, at His right hand, the gift of the Holy Spirit, who was to come down out of the heart of the Father and His everlasting love. And how we have degraded the Holy Spirit into a mere power by which we have to do our work! God forgive us! Oh, that the Holy Spirit might be held in honor as a power to fill us with the very life and nature of God and of Christ!

Christian Work Requires Love

"*The fruit of the Spirit is love.*" Why is it so? And the answer comes: This is the only power in which Christians really can do their work.

Yes, it is love that we need. We need not only love that is to bind us to each other, but we also need a divine love in our work for the lost around us. Oh, do we not often undertake a great deal of work from a natural spirit of compassion for our fellowmen? Do we not often undertake Christian work because our minister or friend calls us to it? And do we not often perform Christian work with a certain zeal but without having had a baptism of love?

People often ask, "What is the baptism of fire?"

I have answered more than once, "I know no fire like the fire of God, the fire of everlasting love that consumed the sacrifice on Calvary." The baptism of love is what the church needs, and to get this we must begin at once to get down on our faces before God in confession, and plead, "Lord, let love from heaven flow down into my heart. I am giving up my life to pray and live as one who has given himself up for the everlasting love to dwell in and fill him."

Ah, yes, if the love of God were in our hearts, what a difference it would make! There are hundreds of believers who say, "I work for Christ, and I feel I could work much harder, but I do not have the gift. I do not know how or where to begin. I do not know what I can do."

Brother, sister, ask God to baptize you with the Spirit of love, and love will find its way. Love is a fire that will burn through every difficulty. You may be a shy, hesitating person who cannot speak well, but love can burn through everything. God fills us with love! We need it for our work.

Perhaps you have read many touching stories of love expressed, and you have said, "How beautiful!" I heard one not long ago. A lady had been asked to speak at a rescue home where there were a number of poor women. As she arrived there and passed by the window with the matron, she saw a wretched woman sitting outside and asked, "Who is that?"

The matron answered, "She has been into the house thirty or forty times, and she has always gone away again. Nothing can be done with her, she is so low and hard."

But the lady said, "She must come in."

The matron then said, "We have been waiting for you, and the company is assembled, and you have only an hour for the address."

The lady replied, "No, this is of more importance," and she went outside where the woman was sitting. She said to the woman, "My sister, what is the matter?"

"I am not your sister," was the reply.

Then the lady laid her hand on her, and said: "Yes, I am your sister, and I love you." So she spoke until the heart of the poor woman was touched.

The conversation lasted some time, and the company was waiting patiently. Ultimately, the lady brought the woman into the room. There was the poor, wretched, degraded creature, full of shame. She would not sit on a chair, but sat down on a stool beside the speaker's seat, and she let her lean against her, with her arms around the poor woman's neck, while she spoke to the assembled people. And that love touched the woman's heart; she had found one who really loved her, and that love gave access to the love of Jesus.

Praise God! There is love on earth in the hearts of God's children; but oh, that there were more!

O God, baptize our ministers with a tender love, and our missionaries, our Bible readers, our workers, and our young men's and young women's associations. Oh, that God would begin with us now and baptize us with heavenly love!

Love Inspires Intercession

Once again, it is only love that can equip us for the work of intercession.

I have said that love must equip us for our work. Do you know what the hardest and the most important work is that has to be done for this sinful world? It is the work of intercession, the work of going to God and taking time to lay hold of Him.

A man may be an earnest Christian, an earnest minister, and he may do good. But unfortunately, how often he has to confess that he knows little of what it is to tarry with God! May God give us the great gift of an intercessory spirit, a spirit of prayer and supplication! Let me ask you in the name of Jesus not to let a day pass without praying for all God's people.

I find that there are Christians who think little of this. I find that there are prayer groups where they pray for the members, and not for all believers. I urge you, take time to pray for the church of Christ. It is right to pray for the heathen, as I have already said. God help us to pray more for them. It is right to pray for missionaries and for evangelistic work and for the unconverted. But Paul did not tell people to pray for the heathen or the unconverted. Paul told them to pray for believers. Make this your first prayer every day: "Lord, bless Your people everywhere."

The state of Christ's church is indescribably low. Plead for God's people that He would visit them, plead for each other, plead for all believers who are trying to work for God. Let love fill your heart. Ask Christ to pour fresh love into you every day. Try to grasp this truth, by the Holy Spirit of God, "I am separated unto the Holy Spirit, and *the fruit of the Spirit is love.*" God help us to understand it.

May God grant that we learn day by day to wait more quietly upon Him. We must not wait upon God only for ourselves, or the power to do so will soon be lost. But we must give ourselves up to the ministry and the love of intercession, and pray more for God's people in general, for God's people around us, for the Spirit of love in ourselves and in them, and for the work of God we are connected with. The answer will surely come, and our waiting upon God will be a source of untold blessing and power. "*The fruit of the Spirit is love.*"

Do you have a lack of love to confess before God? Then make confession and say before Him, "O Lord, my lack of heart, my lack of love—I confess it." And then, as you cast that lack at His feet, believe that the blood cleanses you, that Jesus comes in His mighty, cleansing, saving power to deliver you, and that He will give His Holy Spirit.

"*The fruit of the Spirit is love.*"

3

SEPARATED UNTO THE HOLY SPIRIT

Now in the church that was at Antioch there were certain prophets and teachers: Barnabas, Simeon who was called Niger, Lucius of Cyrene, Manaen…and Saul. As they ministered to the Lord and fasted, the Holy Spirit said, "Now separate to Me Barnabas and Saul for the work to which I have called them." Then, having fasted and prayed, and laid hands on them, they sent them away. So, being sent out by the Holy Spirit, they went down to Seleucia.
—Acts 13:1–4

In the story contained in this Scripture passage, we find some precious thoughts to guide us to what God wants for us, and what God wants to do for us. The great lesson of the verses quoted is this: the Holy Spirit is the director of the work of God upon the earth. And what we should do, if we are to rightly work for God, and if God is to bless our work, is to see that we stand in a right relationship with the Holy Spirit. We must be sure that we give Him the place of honor that belongs to Him everyday. In all our work and (what is more) in our private, inner lives, the Holy Spirit must always have first place. Let me point out to you some of the precious thoughts our passage suggests.

God's Plans for His Kingdom

First of all, we see that God has His own plans with regard to His kingdom. His church at Antioch had been established. God had certain plans and intentions with regard to Asia and with regard to Europe. He had conceived them; they were His, and He made them known to His servants.

Our great Commander organizes every campaign, and His generals and officers do not always know the great plans. They often receive sealed orders, and they have to wait for Him to reveal their contents. God in heaven has wishes and a will in regard to any work that ought to be done, and to the way in which it has to be done. Blessed is the man who receives God's secrets and works under Him.

Some years ago, in Wellington, South Africa, we opened a Mission Institute—what is considered there to be a fine, large building. At our opening services, the principal said something that I have never forgotten. He remarked, "Last year we gathered here to lay the foundation stone, and what was there then to be seen? Nothing but rubbish and stones and bricks and ruins of an old building that had been pulled down. There we laid the foundation stone, and very few knew what the building was that was to rise. No one knew it perfectly in every detail except one man, the architect. In his mind it was all clear, and as the contractor and the mason and the carpenter came to do their work, they took their orders from him. The humblest laborer had to be obedient to orders. The structure rose, and this beautiful building has been completed. And just so," he added, "this building that we open today is simply laying the foundation of a work of which only God knows what is to become."

God has His workers and His plans clearly mapped out. Our position is to wait so that God may communicate to us as much of His will as is necessary.

We simply have to be faithful in obedience, carrying out His orders. God has a plan for His church on earth. But unfortunately, we too often make our own plans. We think that we know what ought to be done. We ask God to bless our feeble efforts, instead of absolutely refusing to go unless God goes before us. God has planned for the work and the extension of His kingdom. The Holy Spirit has had that work given to Him, to be under His control. *"The work to which I have called them."* May God, therefore, help us all to be afraid of touching *"the ark of God"* (2 Samuel 6:6), except as we are led by the Holy Spirit.

God Reveals His Will

Second, God is willing and able to reveal to His servants what His will is.

Yes, blessed be God, communications still come down from heaven! As we read here what the Holy Spirit said, so the Spirit will still speak to His church and His people. In these latter days, He has often done it. He has come to individual men, and by His divine teaching He has led them out into fields of labor that others could not at first understand or approve. He has led them into ways and methods that did not appeal to the majority. But the Holy Spirit still, in our time, teaches His people. Thank God, in our foreign missionary societies and in our home missions, and in a thousand forms of work, the guiding of the Holy Spirit is known. But (we are all ready, I think, to confess) He is too little known. We have not learned to wait upon Him enough, and so we should make a solemn declaration before God: "O God, we need to wait more for You to show us Your will."

Do not ask God only for power. Many Christians have their own plans of working, but God must send the power. The man works in his own will, and God must give the grace—the one reason why God often gives so little grace and so little success. But let us all take our place before God and say, "What is done in the will of God, the strength of God will not be withheld from it. What is done in the will of God must have the mighty blessing of God."

And so let our first desire be to have the will of God revealed.

If you ask me, "Is it an easy thing to get these communications from heaven and to understand them?" I can give you the answer. It is easy to those who are in proper fellowship with heaven, and who understand the art of waiting on God in prayer.

We often ask, "How can a person know the will of God?" And people want, when they are in perplexity, to pray very earnestly so that God will answer them at once. But God can reveal His will only to a heart that is humble and tender and empty. God can reveal His will in perplexities and special difficulties only to a heart that has learned to obey and honor Him loyally in little things and in daily life.

Hearts Surrendered to God

This brings me to the third thought. Note the disposition to which the Spirit reveals God's will.

What do we read in the beginning verses of Acts 13? There were a number of men ministering to the Lord and fasting, and the Holy Spirit came and spoke to them. Some people understand this passage as they would in reference to a missionary committee of our day. We see that there is an open field, and we have had our missions in other fields. We decide to enter that new field. We have virtually settled on this, and we pray about it. But the position was a very different one in those former days. I doubt whether any of them thought of Europe (for later on even Paul himself tried to go back into Asia, until the night vision called him by the will of God). Look at those men. God had done wonders. He had extended the church to Antioch, and He had given rich and large blessings. Now, here were these men ministering to the Lord, serving Him with prayer and fasting. What a deep conviction they had—"It must all come directly from heaven. We are in fellowship with the risen Lord; we must have a close union with Him, and somehow He will let us know what He wants." And there they were, empty, ignorant, helpless, glad, and joyful, but deeply humbled.

"O Lord," they seemed to say, "we are Your servants, and in fasting and prayer we wait upon You. What is Your will for us?"

Was it not the same with Peter? He was on the housetop, fasting and praying, and little did he think of the vision and the command to go to Caesarea. He was ignorant of what his work might be.

It is in hearts entirely surrendered to the Lord Jesus, separating themselves from the world and even from ordinary religious exercises, and giving themselves up in intense prayer to look to their Lord, that the heavenly will of God will be manifested.

The word *fasting* occurs a second time in the third verse: *"Having fasted and prayed."* When you pray, you love to go into your prayer closet, according to the command of Jesus, and shut the door. (See Matthew 6:6.) You shut out business and company and pleasure and anything that can distract, and you want to be alone with God. But in one way, even the material world follows you there. You must eat. These men wanted to shut themselves out from the influences of the material and the visible, and they fasted. What they ate was simply enough to supply the needs of nature. In the intensity of their souls, they thought to give expression to their letting go of everything on earth by fasting before God. Oh, may God give us that intensity of desire—that separation from everything—because we want to wait upon God, so that the Holy Spirit may reveal to us God's blessed will.

Separation unto the Holy Spirit

The fourth thought is this: What is now the will of God as the Holy Spirit reveals it? It is contained in one phrase: separation unto the Holy Spirit. This is the keynote of the message from heaven.

"'*Separate to Me Barnabas and Saul for the work to which I have called them.*' The work is mine; I care for it. I have chosen these men and called them, and I want you who represent the church of Christ upon earth to set them apart unto Me."

Look at this heavenly message in its two aspects. The men were to be set apart to the Holy Spirit, and the church was to do this separating work. The Holy Spirit could trust these men to do it in a right spirit. There they were, abiding in fellowship with the heavenly. The Holy Spirit could say to them, "Do the work of separating these men." And these were the men the Holy Spirit had prepared, and He could say of them, "Let them be separated unto Me."

Here we come to the very root—the very life— of the need of Christian workers. The question is, "What is needed so that the power of God will rest on us more mightily? What is needed so that the blessing of God will be poured out more abundantly among those poor, wretched people and perishing sinners among whom we labor?" And the answer from heaven is, "I want men separated unto the Holy Spirit."

What does this imply? You know that there are two spirits on earth. Christ said, when He spoke about the Holy Spirit, *"The world cannot receive [Him]"* (John 14:17). Paul said, *"We have received, not the spirit of the world, but the Spirit who is from God"* (1 Corinthians 2:12). This is the great need in every worker—the spirit of the world going out, and the Spirit of God coming in to take possession of the inner life and of the whole being.

I am sure there are workers who often cry to God for the Holy Spirit to come upon them as a Spirit of power for their work. When they feel that measure of power, and receive blessing, they thank God for it. But God wants something more and something higher. God wants us to seek the Holy Spirit as a Spirit of power in our own hearts and lives, to conquer self and cast out sin, and to work the blessed and beautiful image of Jesus into us.

There is a difference between the power of the Spirit as a gift and the power of the Spirit for the grace of a holy life. A man may often have a measure of the power of the Spirit, but if there is not a large measure of the Spirit as the Spirit of grace and holiness, the defect will be evident in his work. He may be the means of conversion, but he will never help people on to a higher standard of spiritual life. When he passes away, a great deal of his work may pass away, too. But a man who is separated unto the Holy Spirit is a man who is given up to say, "Father, let the Holy Spirit have full dominion over me, in my home, in my temperament, in every word of my tongue, in every thought of my heart, in every feeling toward my fellowmen. Let the Holy Spirit have entire possession."

Is this what has been the longing and the covenant of your heart with your God—to be a man or a woman separated and given up unto the Holy Spirit? I urge you to listen to the voice of heaven: *"Separate to Me,"* said the Holy Spirit. Yes, separated unto the Holy Spirit. May God grant that the Word may enter into the very depths of our beings to search us, and if we discover that we have not come out from the world entirely—if God discloses to us that self-life, self-will, and self-exaltation are there—let us humble ourselves before Him.

Man, woman, brother, sister, you are a worker separated unto the Holy Spirit. Is this true? Has this been your desire? Has this been your surrender? Has this been what you have expected through faith in the power of our risen and almighty Lord Jesus? If not, here is the call of faith, and here is the key of blessing—separated unto the Holy Spirit. May God write the word in our hearts!

I said that the Holy Spirit spoke to the church in Antioch as a church capable of doing that work. The Holy Spirit trusted them. God grant that our churches, our missionary societies, and all our directors and councils and committees may consist of men and women who are fit for the work of separating workers unto the Holy Spirit. We can ask God for that, too.

A Matter of Action

Then comes my fifth thought: one's holy partnership with the Holy Spirit in this work becomes a matter of consciousness and of action.

These men in Antioch, what did they do? They set apart Paul and Barnabas, and then the two, being sent forth by the Holy Spirit, went to Seleucia. Oh, what fellowship—the Holy Spirit in heaven doing part of the work, men on earth doing the other part! After the ordination of the men on earth, it is written in God's inspired Word that they were sent forth by the Holy Spirit.

See how this partnership called them to new prayer and fasting. They had for a certain time been ministering to the Lord and fasting, perhaps for days. The Holy Spirit spoke, and they had to do the work and enter into partnership, and at once they came together for more prayer and fasting. This is the spirit in which they obeyed the command of their Lord. And this teaches us that it is not only in the beginning of our Christian work, but all along, that we need to have our strength in prayer. If there is one thought with regard to the church of Christ that at times comes to me with overwhelming sorrow; if there is one thought in regard to my own life of which I am ashamed; if there is one thought of which I feel that the church of Christ has not accepted and not grasped; if there is one thought that makes me pray to God, "Oh, teach us new things by Your grace"—it is the wonderful power that prayer is meant to have in the kingdom. We have so little availed ourselves of it.

You may have read the expression of Christian in Bunyan's great work, *The Pilgrim's Progress*, when he found he had the key that would unlock the dungeon. He said, "What a fool am I, thus to lie in a stinking dungeon, when I may as well walk at liberty! I have a key in my bosom, called Promise, that will, I am persuaded, open any lock in Doubting Castle." Similarly, we have the key that can unlock the dungeon of atheism and of heathendom. But, oh, we are far more occupied with our work than we are with prayer! We believe more in speaking to men than we believe in speaking to God. Learn from these men that the work that the Holy Spirit commands must call us to new fasting and prayer, to new separation from the spirit and the pleasures of the world, to new consecration to God and to His fellowship. Those men gave themselves up to fasting and prayer, and if in all our ordinary Christian work there were more prayer, there would be more blessing in our own inner lives. If we felt and proved and testified to the world that our only strength lay in keeping in contact with Christ, every minute allowing Him to work in us—if that were our spirit every minute, would not, by the grace of God, our lives be holier? Would they not be more abundantly fruitful?

I hardly know a more solemn warning in God's Word than that which we find in the third chapter of Galatians, where Paul asked, *"Having begun in the Spirit, are you now being made perfect by the flesh?"* (Galatians 3:3).

Do you understand what this means? A terrible danger in Christian work—just as in a Christian life that is begun with much prayer, begun in the Holy Spirit—is that it may be gradually diverted to the lines of the flesh. In the time of our first perplexity and helplessness, we prayed much to God. God answered and God blessed, and our organization became perfected. Our band of workers became larger. But gradually the organization and the work and the rush have so taken possession of us that the power of the Spirit—in which we began when we were a small company—has almost been lost. Oh, I urge you, note it well! It was with new prayer and fasting, with more prayer and fasting, that this company of disciples carried out the command of the Holy Spirit, *"My soul, wait silently for God alone"* (Psalm 62:5). This is our highest and most important work. The Holy Spirit comes in answer to believing prayer.

When the exalted Jesus had ascended to the throne, the footstool of the throne was the place where His waiting disciples cried to Him for ten days. And this is the law of the kingdom—the King on the throne, the servants on the footstool. May God find us there unceasingly!

The Blessing of the Spirit-Led Life

Here is the final thought: what a wonderful blessing comes when the Holy Spirit is allowed to lead and to direct the work, and when it is carried on in obedience to Him!

You know the story of the mission on which Barnabas and Saul were sent out. You know what power there was with them. The Holy Spirit sent them, and they went on from place to place with large blessing. The Holy Spirit was their leader further on. You recall how it was by the Spirit that Paul was hindered from going again into Asia, and was led away over to Europe. Oh, the blessing that rested on that little company of men and on their ministry unto the Lord!

Let us learn to believe that God has a blessing for us. The Holy Spirit, into whose hands God has put the work, has been called "the Executive of the Holy Trinity." The Holy Spirit has not only power, but He also has the Spirit of love. He is brooding over this dark world and every sphere of work in it, and He is willing to bless. And why is there not more blessing? There can be only one answer. We have not honored the Holy Spirit as we should have done. Is there one who can say that this is not true? Is not every thoughtful heart ready to cry, "God forgive me that I have not honored the Holy Spirit as I should have, that I have grieved Him, that I have allowed self, the flesh, and my own will to work where the Holy Spirit should have been honored! May God forgive me that I have allowed self, the flesh, and the will to actually have the place that God wanted the Holy Spirit to have."

Oh, this sin is greater than we know! No wonder there is so much feebleness and failure in the church of Christ!

4

PETER'S REPENTANCE

And the Lord turned and looked at Peter. And Peter remembered the word of the Lord, how He had said to him, "Before the rooster crows, you will deny Me three times." So Peter went out and wept bitterly.
—Luke 22:61–62

This Scripture describes the turning point in the life of Peter. Christ had said to him, *"You cannot follow Me now"* (John 13:36). Peter was not in a fit state to follow Christ, because he had not been brought to an end of himself. He did not know himself, and he therefore could not follow Christ. But when he went out and wept bitterly, then came the great change. Christ previously said to him, *"When you have returned to Me, strengthen your brethren"* (Luke 22:32).

Here is the point where Peter was converted from self to Christ.

I thank God for the story of Peter. I do not know a man in the Bible who gives us greater comfort. When we look at his character, so full of failures, and at what Christ made him by the power of the Holy Spirit, there is hope for every one of us. But remember, before Christ could fill Peter with the Holy Spirit and make a new man of him, he had to go out and weep bitterly; he had to be humbled. If we want to understand this, I think there are four points that we must look at. First, let us look at Peter, the devoted disciple of Jesus; next, at Peter as he lived the life of self; then, at Peter in his repentance; and last, at what Christ made of Peter by the Holy Spirit.

Peter, the Devoted Disciple of Christ

Christ called Peter to forsake his nets and follow Him. Peter did it at once, and afterward he could rightly say to the Lord, *"We have left all and followed You"* (Matthew 19:27).

Peter was a man of absolute surrender; he gave up all to follow Jesus. Peter was also a man of ready obedience. You remember Christ said to him, *"Launch out into the deep and let down your nets"* (Luke 5:4). Peter, the fisherman, knew there were no fish there, for they had been fishing all night and had caught nothing; but he said, *"At Your word I will let down the net"* (verse 5). He submitted to the word of Jesus. Furthermore, Peter was a man of great faith. When he saw Christ walking on the sea, he said, *"Lord, if it is You, command me to come to You"* (Matthew 14:28). At the voice of Christ, he stepped out of the boat and walked on the water.

Peter was also a man of spiritual insight. When Christ asked the disciples, *"Who do you say that I am?"* Peter was able to answer, *"You are the Christ, the Son of the living God."* And Christ said, *"Blessed are you, Simon Bar-Jonah, for flesh and blood has not revealed this to you, but My Father who is in heaven"* (Matthew 16:15–17). Then Christ spoke of him as the rock, and of his having the keys of the kingdom. (See verses 18–19.) Peter was a splendid man, a devoted disciple of Jesus, and if he were living now, everyone would say that he was an advanced Christian. And yet how much there was lacking in Peter!

Peter, Living the Life of Self

You recall that just after Christ had said to him, *"Flesh and blood has not revealed this to you, but My Father who is in heaven"* (Matthew 16:17), Christ began to speak about His sufferings, and Peter dared to say, *"Far be it from You, Lord; this shall not happen to You!"* (verse 22). Then Christ had to say, *"Get behind Me, Satan! You are an offense to Me, for you are not mindful of the things of God, but the things of men"* (verse 23).

There was Peter in his self-will, trusting his own wisdom, and actually forbidding Christ to go and die. Where did that come from? Peter trusted in himself and his own thoughts about divine things. We see later on, more than once, that the disciples questioned who should be the greatest among them. Peter was one of them, and he thought he had a right to the very first place. He sought his own honor above the others. The life of self was strong in Peter. He had left his boats and his nets, but not his old self.

When Christ had spoken to him about His sufferings, and said, *"Get behind Me, Satan!"* He followed it up by saying: *"If anyone desires to come after Me, let him deny himself, and take up his cross, and follow Me"* (Matthew 16:24). No man can follow Him unless he does this. Self must be utterly denied. What does this mean? We read that when Peter denied Christ, he said three times, *"I do not know Him"* (Luke 22:57). In other words, he said, "I have nothing to do with Him; He and I are not friends. I deny having any connection with Him." Christ told Peter that he must deny self. Self must be ignored, and its every claim rejected. This is the root of true discipleship. But Peter did not understand it and could not obey it. And what happened? When the last night came, Christ said to him, *"Before the rooster crows twice, you will deny Me three times"* (Mark 14:30).

But with self-confidence Peter said, *"Even if all are made to stumble, yet I will not be"* (verse 29). *"Lord, I am ready to go with You, both to prison and to death"* (Luke 22:33).

Peter meant it honestly, and he really intended to do it; but Peter did not know himself. He did not believe he was as bad as Jesus said he was.

We perhaps think of individual sins that come between us and God, but what are we to do with the self-life that is all unclean—our very natures? What are we to do with that flesh that is entirely under the power of sin? Deliverance from this is what we need. Peter did not know it, and therefore it was in self-confidence that he went forth and denied his Lord.

Notice how Christ used the word *deny* twice. He said to Peter the first time, *"Deny himself"* (Matthew 16:24); He said to Peter the second time, *"You will deny Me"* (Matthew 26:34). It is either of the two. There is no other choice for us; we must either deny self or deny Christ. There are two great powers fighting each other—the self-nature in the power of sin, and Christ in the power of God. One of these must rule within us.

It was self that made the devil. He was an angel of God, but he wanted to exalt self. He became a devil in hell. Self was the cause of the fall of man. Eve wanted something for herself, and so our first parents fell into all the wretchedness of sin. We, their children, have inherited an awful nature of sin.

Peter's Repentance

Peter denied his Lord three times, and then the Lord looked upon him. That look of Jesus broke

Peter's heart. The terrible sin that he had committed, the terrible failure that had come, and the depth into which he had fallen suddenly opened up before him. Then, Peter *"went out and wept bitterly."*

Oh, who can tell what that repentance must have been? During the following hours of that night and the next day—when he saw Christ crucified and buried, and the next day, the Sabbath—oh, what hopeless despair and shame he must have felt!

"My Lord is gone; my hope is gone; and I denied my Lord. After that life of love, after that blessed fellowship of three years, I denied my Lord. God have mercy upon me!"

I do not think we can imagine the depth of humiliation Peter sank into then. But that was the turning point and the change. On the first day of the week, Christ was seen by Peter, and in the evening He met him with the others. Later on at the Sea of Galilee, He asked him, *"Do you love Me?"* (John 21:17). Peter was made sad by the thought that the Lord reminded him of having denied Him three times, and said in sorrow, but in uprightness, *"Lord, You know all things; You know that I love You"* (verse 17).

Peter Transformed

Now, Peter was prepared for deliverance from self, and this is my last thought. You know that Christ took him with the others to the footstool of the throne and told them to wait there. Then, on the Day of Pentecost, the Holy Spirit came, and Peter was a changed man. I do not want you to think only of the change in Peter, in that boldness, that power, that insight into the Scriptures, and that blessing with which he preached that day. Thank God for that. But there was something deeper and better that happened to Peter. His whole nature was changed. The work that Christ began in Peter when He looked upon him was perfected when he was filled with the Holy Spirit.

If you want to see this, read the first epistle of Peter. You know where Peter's failings lay. When he said to Christ, in effect, "You can never suffer; it cannot be," it showed he did not have an idea of what it was to pass through death into life. Christ said, "Deny yourself," and in spite of this he denied his Lord. When Christ warned him, *"You will deny Me"* (Matthew 26:34), and he insisted that he never would, Peter showed how little he understood what there was in himself.

But when I read his epistle in which he said, *"If you are reproached for the name of Christ, blessed are you, for the Spirit of glory and of God rests upon you"* (1 Peter 4:14), then I say that it is not the old Peter, but it is the very Spirit of Christ breathing and speaking within him.

I read again how Peter said, *"You were called [to suffer], because Christ also suffered for us"* (1 Peter 2:21). I understand what a change had come over Peter. Instead of denying Christ, he found joy and pleasure in having self denied, crucified, and given up to the death. And therefore, we read in Acts that when he was called before the council he could boldly say, *"We ought to obey God rather than men"* (Acts 5:29), and that he could return with the other disciples and rejoice that they were counted worthy to suffer for Christ's name. (See verse 41.)

You remember his self-exaltation; but now he had found out that *"the incorruptible beauty of a gentle and quiet spirit…is very precious in the sight of God"* (1 Peter 3:4). Again he told us to be *"be submissive to one another, and be clothed with humility"* (1 Peter 5:5).

Dear friend, I implore you, look at Peter utterly changed—the self-pleasing, the self-trusting, the self-seeking Peter, full of sin, continually getting into trouble, foolish and impetuous, now filled with the Spirit and the life of Jesus. Christ had done it for him by the Holy Spirit.

And now, what is the point in my having thus pointed to the story of Peter? This story must be the story of every believer who is really to be made a blessing by God. This story is a prophecy of what everyone can receive from God in heaven.

Now, let us just glance at what these lessons teach us.

The first lesson is this: you may be a very earnest, godly, devoted believer, in whom the power of the flesh is still very strong.

This is a very solemn truth. Peter, before he denied Christ, had cast out devils and had healed the sick. Yet the flesh had power, and the flesh had room in him. Oh, beloved, we have to realize that it is because there is so much of the self-life in us that the power of God cannot work in us as mightily as He desires it to work. Do you realize that the great God is longing to double His blessing, to give tenfold blessing through us? But there is something hindering Him, and that something is nothing but the self-life. We talk about the pride of Peter, and the impetuosity of Peter, and the self-confidence of Peter. It is all rooted in that one word, *self*. Christ had said, "Deny self," and Peter had never understood and never obeyed. Every failing came out of that.

What a solemn thought, and what an urgent plea for us to cry, "Oh God, show this to us so that none of us may be living the self-life!" It has happened to people who have been Christians for years; it has happened to people who have perhaps occupied prominent positions—God found them out and taught them to find out about themselves. They became utterly ashamed and fell broken before God. Oh, the bitter shame and sorrow and pain and agony that came to them, until at last they found that there was deliverance! Peter *"went out and wept bitterly."* There may be many godly people in whom the power of the flesh still rules.

My second lesson is this: it is the work of our blessed Lord Jesus to disclose the power of self.

How was it that Peter—the carnal Peter, self-willed Peter, Peter with the strong self-love—ever became a man of Pentecost and the writer of his epistles? It was because Christ placed him in charge, and Christ watched over him, and Christ taught and blessed him.

The warnings that Christ had given him were part of the training. Last of all, there came that look of love. In His suffering, Christ did not forget him, but turned around and looked upon him, and Peter *"went out and wept bitterly."* And the Christ who led Peter to Pentecost is waiting today to take charge of every heart that is willing to surrender itself to Him.

Are there not some people saying, "Ah, that is the problem with me! It is always the self-life, self-comfort, self-consciousness, self-pleasing, and self-will. How am I to get rid of it?"

My answer is, It is Christ Jesus who can rid you of it. No one else but Christ Jesus can give deliverance from the power of self. And what does He ask you to do? He asks that you humble yourself before Him.

5

IMPOSSIBLE WITH MAN, POSSIBLE WITH GOD

But He said, "The things which are impossible with men are possible with God."
—Luke 18:27

Christ had said to the rich young ruler, *"Sell all that you have…and come, follow Me"* (Luke 18:22). The young man went away sorrowful. Christ then turned to the disciples and said, *"How hard it is for those who have riches to enter the kingdom of God!"* (verse 24). The disciples, we read, were greatly astonished and answered, *"Who then can be saved?"* (verse 26). And Christ gave this blessed answer, *"The things which are impossible with men are possible with God."*

The text contains two thoughts: first, that in the question of salvation and of following Christ by a holy life, it is impossible for man to do it; second, that what is impossible with man is possible with God.

These two thoughts mark the two great lessons that one has to learn in the Christian life. It often takes a long time to learn the first lesson—that in the Christian life man can do nothing, that salvation is impossible to man. And often a man learns this, and yet he does not learn the second lesson—that what has been impossible to him is possible with God. Blessed is the man or woman who learns both lessons! The learning of them marks stages in the Christian's life.

Man Cannot

The one stage is when a man is trying to do his utmost and fails, when a man tries to do better and fails again, when a man tries much more and always fails. And yet, very often he does not even then learn the lesson: with man it is impossible to serve God and Christ. Peter spent three years in Christ's school, and he never learned that it is impossible, until he had denied his Lord and *"went out and wept bitterly"* (Luke 22:62). Then he learned it.

Just look for a moment at a person who is learning this lesson. At first, he fights against it. Then he submits to it, but reluctantly and in despair. At last, he accepts it willingly and rejoices in it. At the beginning of the Christian life, the young convert has no idea of this truth. He has been converted; he has the joy of the Lord in his heart; he begins to run the race and fight the battle. He is sure he can conquer, for he is earnest and honest, and God will help him. Yet somehow, very soon he fails where he did not expect it, and sin gets the better of him. He is disappointed, but he thinks, "I was not cautious enough. I did not make my resolutions strong enough." And again he vows, and again he prays, and yet he fails. He thinks, "Am I not a redeemed man? Have I not the life of God within me?" And he thinks again, "Yes, and I have Christ to help me. I can live the holy life."

At a later period, he comes to another state of mind. He begins to see such a life is impossible, but he does not accept it. There are multitudes of Christians who come to this point: "I cannot." They then think that God never expected them to do what they cannot do. If you tell them that God does expect it, it is a mystery to them. A good many Christians are living a low life—a life of failure and of sin—instead of rest and victory, because they began to say, "I cannot, it is impossible." And yet they do not understand it fully. So, under the impression of "I cannot," they give way to despair. They will do their best, but they never expect to get very far.

But God leads His children on to a third stage. A man comes to accept "it is impossible" in its full truth, and yet at the same time says, "I must do it, and I will do it. It is impossible for man, and yet I must do it." The renewed will begins to exercise its whole power, and in intense longing and prayer begins to cry to God, "Lord, what is the meaning of this? How am I to be freed from the power of sin?"

This is the state of the regenerate man in Romans 7. There you will find the Christian man trying his very utmost to live a holy life. God's law has been revealed to him as reaching down into the very depth of the desires of the heart. The man can dare to say, "*I delight in the law of God according to the inward man* (Romans 7:22).... *To will* [what is good] *is present with me*" (verse 18). My heart loves the law of God, and my will has chosen that law."

Can a man like this fail, with his heart full of delight in God's law and with his will determined to do what is right? Yes. This is what Romans 7 teaches us. There is something more needed. Not only must I delight in *"the law of God according to the inward man"* (Romans 7:22) and will what God wills, but I need a divine omnipotence to work it in me. And this is what the apostle Paul taught in Philippians 2:13: *"It is God who works in you both to will and to do for His good pleasure."*

Note the contrast. In Romans 7, the regenerate man says, *"To will is present with me, but how to perform what is good I do not find"* (verse 18). But in Philippians 2, you have a man who has been led on farther. He is a man who understands that when God has worked the renewed will, He will give the power to accomplish what that will desires. Let us receive this as the first great lesson in the spiritual life: "It is impossible for me, my God. Let there be an end of the flesh and all its powers, an end of self, and let it be my glory to be helpless."

Praise God for the divine teaching that makes us helpless! When you thought of absolute surrender to God, were you not brought to an end of yourself? Did you not feel that you could see how you actually could live as a man absolutely surrendered to God every moment of the day—at your table, in your house, in your business, in the midst of trials and temptations? I pray that you will learn the lesson now. If you felt you could not do it, you are on the right road if you let yourselves be led. Accept this position, and maintain it before God: "My heart's desire and delight, O God, is absolute surrender, but I cannot perform it. It is impossible for me to live that life. It is beyond me." Fall down and learn that when you are utterly helpless, God will come to work in you not only to will, but also to do.

God Can

Now comes the second lesson: the things that are impossible with men are possible with God.

I said a little while ago that there is many a man who has learned the lesson that it is impossible with men, and then he gives up in helpless despair. He lives a wretched Christian life, without joy or strength or victory. And why? Because he does not humble himself to learn that other lesson: with God all things are possible.

Your Christian life is to be a continuous proof that God works impossibilities. Your Christian life is to be a series of impossibilities made possible and actual by God's almighty power. This is what the Christian needs. He has an almighty God whom he worships, and he must learn to understand that he does not need a little of God's power. Rather—and I say this with reverence—he needs the whole of God omnipotence to keep him right and to live like a Christian.

The whole of Christianity is a work of God's omnipotence. Look at the birth of Christ Jesus. That was a miracle of divine power, and it was said to Mary, *"With God nothing will be impossible"* (Luke 1:37). It was the omnipotence of God. Look at Christ's resurrection. We are taught that it was according to the *"exceeding greatness of…His mighty power"* (Ephesians 1:19) that God raised Christ from the dead.

Every tree must grow on the root from which it springs. An oak tree three hundred years old grows all the time on the one root from which it had its beginning. Christianity had its beginning in the omnipotence of God. In every soul, Christianity must have its continuance in that omnipotence. All the possibilities of the higher Christian life have their origin in a new understanding of Christ's power to work all God's will in us.

I want to call on you now to come and worship an almighty God. Have you learned to do it? Have you learned to deal so closely with an almighty God that you know omnipotence is working in you? In outward appearance there is often little sign of it. The apostle Paul said, "*I was with you in weakness, in fear, and in much trembling. And…my preaching* [was] *in demonstration of the Spirit and of power*" (1 Corinthians 2:3–4). From the human side there was feebleness; from the divine side there was divine omnipotence. And this is true of every godly life. If we would only learn this lesson better, and give a wholehearted, undivided surrender to it, we would learn what blessedness there is in dwelling every hour and every moment with an almighty God. Have you ever studied in the Bible the attribute of God's omnipotence? You know that it was God's omnipotence that created the world, and created light out of darkness, and created man. But have you studied God's omnipotence in the works of redemption?

Look at Abraham. When God called him to be the father of the people out of which Christ was to be born, He said to him, "*I am Almighty God; walk before me and be blameless*" (Genesis 17:1). And God trained

Abraham to trust Him as the omnipotent One. Whether it was his going out to a land that he did not know, or his faith as a pilgrim amid the thousands of Canaanites, his faith said, "This is my land." Whether it was his faith in waiting twenty-five years for a son in his old age, against all hope, or whether it was the raising up of Isaac from the dead on Mount Moriah when he was going to sacrifice him, Abraham believed God. He was *"strengthened in faith, giving glory to God, and being fully convinced that what He had promised He was also able to perform"* (Romans 4:20–21).

The cause of the weakness of your Christian life is that you want to work it out partly, and to let God help you. And that cannot be. You must come to be utterly helpless, to let God work. He will work gloriously. This is what we need if we are indeed to be workers for God. I could go through Scripture and prove to you how Moses, when he led Israel out of Egypt—how Joshua, when he brought them into the land of Canaan—how all God's servants in the Old Testament counted on the omnipotence of God doing impossibilities. And this God lives today; this God is the God of every child of His. Yet some of us want God to give us a little help while we do our best, instead of coming to understand what God wants, and to say, "I can do nothing. God must and will do all." Have you said, "In worship, in work, in sanctification, in obedience to God, I can do nothing of myself, and so my place is to worship God, and to believe that He will work in me every moment"? Oh, may God teach us this! Oh, that God would by His grace show you what a God you have, and to what a God you have entrusted yourself—an omnipotent God. He is willing, with His whole omnipotence, to place Himself at the disposal of every child of His! Will we not take the lesson of the Lord Jesus and say, "Amen; the things that are impossible with men are possible with God"?

Remember what I have said about Peter, his self-confidence, self-power, self-will, and how he came to deny his Lord. You feel, "Ah, there is the self-life; there is the flesh-life that rules in me!" And now, have you believed that there is deliverance from it? Have you believed that Almighty God is able to reveal Christ in your heart, to let the Holy Spirit rule in you so that the self-life will not have power or dominion over you? Have you coupled the two together and, with tears of repentance and with deep humiliation and feebleness, cried out, "O God, it is impossible to me; man cannot do it, but glory to Your name, it is possible with God"? Have you claimed deliverance? Do it now. Put yourself afresh in absolute surrender into the hands of a God of infinite love. His power to do it is as infinite as His love.

God Works in Man

But again, we come to the question of absolute surrender and feel that that is lacking in the church of Christ. This is why the Holy Spirit cannot fill us, and why we cannot live as people entirely separated unto the Holy Spirit. This is why the flesh and the self-life cannot be conquered. We have never understood what it is to be absolutely surrendered to God as Jesus was. I know that many earnestly and honestly say, "Amen, I accept the message of absolute surrender to God." Yet they think, "Will that ever be mine? Can I count on God to make me one of whom it will be said in heaven, on earth, and in hell, 'He lives in absolute surrender to God'?" Brother, sister, *the things which are impossible with men are possible with God.*" Believe that, when He takes charge of you in Christ, it is possible for God to make you a man or woman of absolute surrender. And God is able to maintain this. He is able to let you rise from bed every morning of the week with this blessed thought, directly or indirectly: "I am in God's care. My God is working out my life for me."

Some of you are weary of thinking about sanctification. You pray; you have longed and cried for it; and yet, it has appeared so far off! You are so conscious of how distant the holiness and humility of Jesus is. Beloved friends, the one doctrine of sanctification that is scriptural and real and effective is this: *"The things which are impossible with men are possible with God."* God can sanctify men. By His almighty and sanctifying power, God can keep them every moment. Oh, that we might get a step nearer to our God now! Oh, that the light of God might shine, and that we might know our God better!

I could go on to speak about the life of Christ in us—living like Christ, taking Christ as our Savior from sin, and as our life and strength. It is God in heaven who can reveal this in you. The prayer of the apostle Paul was, *"That He would grant you, according to the riches of His glory, to be strengthened with might through His Spirit in the inner man"* (Ephesians 3:16). Do you not see that it is an omnipotent God working by His omnipotence in the heart of His believing children, so that Christ can become an indwelling Savior? You have tried to grasp it, to understand it, and to believe it, and it would not come. It was because you had not been brought to believe that *the things which are impossible with men are possible with God.*

And so I trust that the word spoken about love may have brought many to see that we must have an inflowing of love in quite a new way. Our hearts must be filled with life from above—from the fountain of everlasting love—if they are going to overflow all day. Then it will be just as natural for us to love our fellowmen as it is natural for the lamb to be gentle and the wolf to be cruel. When we are brought to such a state that the more a man hates and speaks evil of us—the more unlikable and unlovable a man is, we will love him all the more. When we are brought to such a state that obstacles, hatred, and ingratitude surround us, the power of love can triumph in us all the more. Until you are brought to see these, you are not saying: "It is impossible with men." But if you have been led to say, "This message has spoken to you about a love utterly beyond my power. It is absolutely impossible," then you can come to God and say, "It is possible with You."

Some people are crying to God for a great revival. I can say that this is the unceasing prayer of my heart. Oh, if God would only revive His believing people! I cannot think of the unconverted formalists of the church or of the infidels and skeptics or of all the wretched and perishing around me, without my heart pleading, "My God, revive Your church and people." It is not for a lack of reason that thousands of hearts yearn after holiness and consecration. It is a forerunner of God's power. God works to will and then He works to do. (See Philippians 2:13.) These yearnings are a witness and a proof that God has worked to will. Oh, let us in faith believe that the omnipotent God will work to do among His people more than we can ask. Paul said, *"Now to Him who is able to do exceedingly abundantly above all that we ask or think,…to Him be glory"* (Ephesians 3:20–21). Let our hearts say this. Glory to God, the omnipotent One, who can do above what we dare to ask or think!

"The things which are impossible with men are possible with God." All around you there is a world of sin and sorrow, and Satan is there. But remember, Christ is on the throne; Christ is stronger; Christ has conquered, and Christ will conquer. But wait on God.

My text casts us down—*"The things which are impossible with men"*—but it ultimately lifts us up high—*"are possible with God."* Get linked to God. Adore and trust Him as the omnipotent One, not only for your own life, but for all the souls that are entrusted to you. Never pray without adoring His omnipotence, saying, "Mighty God, I claim Your almightiness." And the answer to the prayer will come. Like Abraham you will become strong in faith, giving glory to God, because you know that He who has promised is able to perform. (See Romans 4:20–21.)

6

OUT OF BONDAGE

> *O wretched man that I am!*
> *Who will deliver me from this body of death?*
> *I thank God; through Jesus Christ our Lord!*
> —Romans 7:24–25

Y ou know the wonderful location that this text has in the epistle to the Romans. It stands here at the end of the seventh chapter as the gateway into the eighth. In the first sixteen verses of the eighth chapter, the name of the Holy Spirit is found sixteen times. You have there the description and promise of the life that a child of God can live in the power of the Holy Spirit. This begins in the second verse: *"For the law of the Spirit of life in Christ Jesus has made me free from the law of sin and death"* (Romans 8:2). From this, Paul went on to speak of the great privileges of the child of God who is led by the Spirit of God. The gateway into all this is found at the end of chapter seven: "*O wretched man that I am!*" Here you have the words of a man who has come to the end of himself. He had in the previous verses described how he had struggled and wrestled in his own power to obey the holy law of God, and had failed. But in answer to his own questions, he now found the true answer and cried out, "*I thank God; through Jesus Christ our Lord!*" From that he went on to speak of the deliverance that he had found.

From these words, I want to describe the path by which a man can be led out of the spirit of bondage into the spirit of liberty. You know how distinctly it is said, "*You did not receive the spirit of bondage again to fear*" (Romans 8:15). We are continually warned that this is the great danger of the Christian life, to go again into bondage. I want to describe the path by which a man can get out of bondage into the glorious liberty of the children of God. Rather, I want to describe the man himself.

First, these words are the language of a regenerate man; second, of a weak man; third, of a wretched man; and fourth, of a man on the border of complete liberty.

The Regenerate Man

There is much evidence of regeneration from the fourteenth verse of chapter seven on to the twenty-third verse. *"It is no longer I who do it, but sin that dwells in me"* (Romans 7:17). This is the language of a regenerate man—a man who knows that his heart and nature have been renewed, and that sin is now a power in him that is not himself. *"I delight in the law of God according to the inward man"* (verse 22). This, again, is the language of a regenerate man. He dares to say when he does evil, *"It is no longer I who do it, but sin that dwells in me."* It is of great importance to understand this.

In the first two sections of the epistle, Paul dealt with justification and sanctification. In dealing with justification, he lay the foundation of the doctrine in the teaching about sin. He did not speak of the singular *sin*, but of the plural *sins*—the actual transgressions. In the second part of the fifth chapter, he began to deal with sin, not as actual transgression, but as a power. Just imagine what a loss it would have been to us if we did not have this second half of the seventh chapter of the epistle to the Romans—if Paul had omitted from his teaching this vital question of the sinfulness of the believer. We would have missed the question we all want answered regarding sin in the believer. What is the answer? The regenerate man is one in whom the will has been renewed, and who can say, *"I delight in the law of God according to the inward man"* (Romans 7:22).

The Weak Man

Here is the great mistake made by many Christian people: they think that when there is a renewed will, it is enough. But this is not the case. This regenerate man tells us, "I will to do what is good, but I do not have the power to perform." How often people tell us that if you set yourself determinedly, you can perform what you will! But this man was as determined as any man can be, and yet he made the confession: *"To will is present with me, but how to perform what is good I do not find"* (Romans 7:18).

But, you ask, "How does God make a regenerate man utter such a confession? He has a right will, a heart that longs to do good, and he longs to do his very utmost to love God."

Let us look at this question. What has God given us our wills for? Did the angels who fell, in their own wills, have the strength to stand? Surely, no. The will of man is nothing but an empty vessel in which the power of God is to be manifested. Man must seek in God all that is to be. You have it in the second chapter of the epistle to the Philippians, and you have it here also, that God's work is to work in us both to will and to do of His good pleasure. Here is a man who appears to say, "God has not worked to do in me." But we are taught that God works both to will and to do. How is the apparent contradiction to be reconciled?

You will find that in this passage (see Romans 7:6–25), the name of the Holy Spirit does not occur once, nor does the name of Christ occur. The man is wrestling and struggling to fulfill God's law. Instead of the Holy Spirit and Christ, the law is mentioned nearly twenty times. This chapter shows a believer doing his very best to obey the law of God with his regenerate will. Not only this, but you will find the little words *I*, *me*, and *my* occur more than forty times. It is the regenerate *I* in its weakness seeking to obey the law without being filled with the Spirit. This is the experience of nearly every believer. After conversion, a person begins to do his best, and he fails. But if we are brought into the full light, we no longer need to fail. Nor do we need to fail at all if we have received the Spirit in His fullness at conversion.

God allows this failure so that the regenerate man will be taught his own utter inability. It is in the course of this struggle that the sense of our utter sinfulness comes to us. It is God's way of dealing with us. He allows man to strive to fulfill the law so that, as he strives and wrestles, he may be brought to say, "I am a regenerate child of God, but I am utterly helpless to obey His law." See what strong words are used all through the chapter to describe this condition: *"I am carnal, sold under sin"* (Romans 7:14); *"I see another law in my members,…bringing me into captivity"* (verse 23); and last of all, *"O wretched man that I am! Who will deliver me from this body of death?"* This believer who bows here in deep contrition is utterly unable to obey the law of God.

The Wretched Man

Not only is the man who makes this confession a regenerate and a weak man, but he is also a wretched man. He is utterly unhappy and miserable. What is it that makes him so utterly miserable? It is because God has given him a nature that loves Himself. He is deeply wretched because he feels he is not obeying his God. He says, with brokenness of heart, "It is not I that do it, but I am under the awful power of sin, which is holding me down. It is I, and yet not I. Alas! It is myself; so closely am I bound up with it, and so closely is it intertwined with my very nature." Blessed be God; when a man learns to say, "*O wretched man that I am!*" from the depth of his heart, he is on the way to the eighth chapter of Romans.

There are many who make this confession an excuse for sin. They say that if Paul had to confess his weakness and helplessness in this way, who are they that they should try to do better? So the call to holiness is quietly set aside. Pray God that every one of us would learn to say these words in the very spirit in which they are written here! When we hear sin spoken of as the abominable thing that God hates, do not many of us wince before the word? If only all Christians who go on sinning and sinning would take this verse to heart. If ever you utter a sharp word say, "*O wretched man that I am!*" And every time you lose your temper, kneel down and understand that God never meant His child to remain in this state. If only we would take this word into our daily lives, and say it every time we see that we have sought our own honor! If only we would take it into our hearts every time we say sharp things, and every time we sin against the Lord God, and against the Lord Jesus Christ in His humility, obedience, and self-sacrifice! Pray God that we could forget everything else and cry out, "*O wretched man that I am! Who will deliver me from this body of death?*"

Why should you say this whenever you commit sin? Because it is when a man is brought to this confession that deliverance is at hand.

And remember, it was not only the sense of being weak and taken captive that made him wretched. It was, above all, the sense of sinning against his God. The law was doing its work, making sin exceedingly sinful in his sight. The thought of continually grieving God became utterly unbearable. It was this that brought forth the piercing cry, "*O wretched man!*" As long as we talk and reason about our inability and our failure, and only try to find out what Romans 7 means, it will profit us little. But when every sin gives new intensity to the sense of wretchedness, and we feel our whole state as one of not only helplessness, but actual and great sinfulness, we will be moved not only to ask, *"Who will deliver me?"* but also to cry, *"I thank God; through Jesus Christ my Lord!"*

The Almost-Delivered Man

The man has tried to obey the beautiful law of God. He has loved it; he has wept over his sin; and he has tried to conquer. He has tried to overcome fault after fault, but every time he has ended in failure.

What did he mean by *"this body of death"*? Did he mean, "my body when I die"? Surely not. In the eighth chapter, you have the answer to this question in the words, *"If by the Spirit you put to death the deeds of the body, you will live"* (Romans 8:13). This is the body of death from which he is seeking deliverance.

And now he is on the brink of deliverance! In the twenty-third verse of the seventh chapter, we have the words, *"I see another law in my members, warring against the law of my mind, and bringing me into captivity to the law of sin which is in my members."* It is a captive who cries, *"O wretched man that I am! Who will deliver me from this body of death?"* He is a man who feels himself bound. But look to the contrast in the second verse of the eighth chapter: *"The law of the Spirit of life in Christ Jesus has made me free from the law of sin and death."* This is the deliverance through Jesus Christ our Lord, the liberty to the captive that the Spirit brings. Can you keep captive any longer a man made free by the *"law of the Spirit of life in Christ Jesus"*?

But you say that the regenerate man did not have the Spirit of Jesus when he spoke in the sixth chapter. Yes, he did not know what the Holy Spirit could do for him.

God does not work by His Spirit as He works by a blind force in nature. He leads His people on as reasonable, intelligent beings. Therefore, when He wants to give us the Holy Spirit whom He has promised, He first brings us to the end of self. He brings us to the conviction that although we have been striving to obey the law, we have failed. When we have come to the end of that, then He shows us that in the Holy Spirit we have the power of obedience, the power of victory, and the power of real holiness.

God works to will, and He is ready to work to do, but many Christians misunderstand this. They think because they have the will, it is enough, and that now they are able to do. This is not so. The new will is a permanent gift, an attribute of the new nature. The power to do is not a permanent gift, but must be received each moment from the Holy Spirit. It is the man who is conscious of his own weakness as a believer who will learn that by the Holy Spirit he can live a holy life. This man is on the brink of that great deliverance; the way has been prepared for the glorious eighth chapter. I now ask this solemn question: Where are you living? With you, is it, *"O wretched man that I am! Who will deliver me?"* with a little experience of the power of the Holy Spirit every now and then? Or is it, *"I thank God; through Jesus Christ!…The law of the Spirit…has made me free from the law of sin and of death"*?

What the Holy Spirit does is to give the victory. *"If by the Spirit you put to death the deeds of the body, you will live"* (Romans 8:13). It is the Holy Spirit who does this—the third person of the Godhead. It is He who, when the heart is opened wide to receive Him, comes in and reigns there, and mortifies the deeds of the body, day by day, hour by hour, and moment by moment.

I want to bring this to a point. Remember, dear friend, what we need is to come to decision and action. In Scripture there are two very different sorts of Christians; one is led by the flesh, the other by the Spirit. The Bible speaks in Romans, Corinthians, and Galatians about yielding to the flesh, and this is the life of tens of thousands of believers. All their lack of joy in the Holy Spirit, and their lack of the liberty He gives, is just owing to the flesh. The Spirit is within them, but the flesh rules the life. To be led by the Spirit of God is what they need. If only I could make every child of His realize what it means that the everlasting God has given His dear Son, Christ Jesus, to watch over you every day, and that what you have to do is to trust. If only I could make His children understand that the work of the Holy Spirit is to enable you every moment to remember Jesus and to trust Him! The Spirit has come to keep the link with Him unbroken every moment. Praise God for the Holy Spirit! We are so accustomed to thinking of the Holy Spirit as a luxury for special times or for special ministers and men. But the Holy Spirit is necessary for every believer, every moment of the day. Praise God that you have Him, and that He gives you the full experience of the deliverance in Christ as He makes you free from the power of sin.

Who longs to have the power and the liberty of the Holy Spirit? Oh, brother or sister, bow before God in one final cry of despair: "O God, must I go on sinning this way forever? Who will deliver me, O wretched man that I am, from this body of death?"

Are you ready to sink before God in that cry and to seek the power of Jesus to live and work in you? Are you ready to say, "*I thank God; through Jesus Christ*"?

What good does it do that we go to church or attend conventions, that we study our Bibles and pray, unless our lives are filled with the Holy Spirit? This is what God wants. Nothing else will enable us to live a life of power and peace. How sad that many Christians are content with the question, "*Who will deliver me from this body of death?*" but never give the answer. Instead of answering, they are silent. Instead of saying, "*I thank God; through Jesus Christ our Lord,*" they are forever repeating the question without the answer. If you want the path to the full deliverance of Christ and the liberty of the Spirit—the glorious liberty of the children of God—take it through the seventh chapter of Romans. Then say, "*I thank God; through Jesus Christ our Lord!*" Do not be content to remain ever groaning, but say, "I, a wretched man or woman, thank God through Jesus Christ. Even though I do not see it all, I am going to praise God."

Here is deliverance; here is the liberty of the Holy Spirit. The kingdom of God is *"joy in the Holy Spirit"* (Romans 14:17).

7

LIVING IN THE SPIRIT

*This only I want to learn from you: Did you receive the
Spirit by the works of the law, or by the hearing of faith?
Are you so foolish? Having begun in the Spirit, are you
now being made perfect by the flesh?*
—Galatians 3:2–3

When we speak of the quickening or the deepening or the strengthening of the spiritual life, we are speaking of something that is feeble and wrong and sinful. It is a great thing to take our place before God with the confession. "O God, my spiritual life is not what it should be!" May God work that in your heart, dear reader.

As we look at the church, we see so many indications of feebleness, failure, sin, and shortcoming. They compel us to ask, Why is it? Is there any necessity for the church of Christ to be living in such a low state? Or is it actually possible that God's people should be living always in the joy and strength of their God?

Every believing heart must answer, It is possible.

Then comes the great question, How is it to be accounted for, that God's church as a whole is so feeble, and that the great majority of Christians are not living up to their privileges? There must be a reason for it. Has God not given Christ His almighty Son to be the Keeper of every believer, to make Christ an ever-present reality, and to impart and communicate to us all that we have in Christ? God has given His Son, and God has given His Spirit. How is it that believers do not live up to their privileges?

In more than one of the epistles, we find a very solemn answer to this question. There are epistles, such as the first to the Thessalonians, where Paul wrote to the Christians, in effect, "I want you to grow, to abound, to increase more and more." They were young, and there were things lacking in their faith. But their state was so far satisfactory, and gave him such great joy, that he wrote time after time, "*We urge and exhort in the Lord Jesus that you should abound more and more*"

(1 Thessalonians 4:1); *"We urge you, brethren, that you increase more and more"* (verse 10). But there are other epistles where he took a very different tone, especially the epistles to the Corinthians and to the Galatians, and he told them in many different ways what the one reason was that they were not living as Christians ought to live: many were under the power of the flesh. Our text verse is one example. Paul reminded them that they had received the Holy Spirit by the preaching of faith. He had preached Christ to them; they had accepted Christ and had received the Holy Spirit in power.

But what happened? They tried to perfect the work that the Spirit had begun in the flesh by their own efforts. We find the same teaching in the epistle to the Corinthians.

Now, we have here a solemn revelation of what the great need is in the church of Christ. God has called the church of Christ to live in the power of the Holy Spirit. But the church is living, for the most part, in the power of human flesh, and of will and energy and effort apart from the Spirit of God. I do not doubt that this is the case with many individual believers. And oh, if God will use me to give you a message from Him, my one message will be this: If the church will acknowledge that the Holy Spirit is her strength and her help, and if the church will give up everything and wait on God to be filled with the Spirit, her days of beauty and gladness will return. We will see the glory of God revealed among us. This is my message to every individual believer: Nothing will help you unless you come to understand that you must live every day under the power of the Holy Spirit.

God wants you to be a living vessel in whom the power of the Spirit is manifested every hour and every moment of your life. God will enable you to be this.

Now, let us try to learn what this word to the Galatians teaches us—some very simple thoughts. It shows us, first, that the beginning of the Christian life is receiving the Holy Spirit. Second, it shows us what great danger there is of forgetting that we are to live by the Spirit and not live according to the flesh. It shows us, third, what are the fruits and the proofs of our seeking perfection in the flesh. And then it suggests to us, finally, the way of deliverance from this state.

Receiving the Holy Spirit

First of all, Paul said, *"Having begun in the Spirit."* Remember, the apostle not only preached justification by faith, but he preached something more. He preached—the epistle is full of it—that justified men cannot live except by the Holy Spirit, and that therefore God gives to every justified man the Holy Spirit to seal him. The apostle said to them, in effect, more than once, "How did you receive the Holy Spirit? Was it by the preaching of the law, or by the preaching of faith?"

He could point back to that time when there had been a mighty revival under his teaching. The power of God had been manifested, and the Galatians were compelled to confess, "Yes, we have the Holy Spirit; we accepted Christ by faith, and by faith we received the Holy Spirit."

Now, it is to be feared that there are many Christians who hardly know that when they believed, they received the Holy Spirit. A great many Christians can say, "I received pardon, and I received peace." But if you were to ask them, "Have you received the Holy Spirit?" they would hesitate. And many, if they were to say yes, would say it with hesitation. They would tell you that they hardly know what it is, since that time, to walk in the power of the Holy Spirit. Let us try to take hold of this great truth: the beginning of the true

Christian life is to receive the Holy Spirit. And the work of every Christian minister is that which was the work of Paul—to remind his people that they received the Holy Spirit, and must live according to His guidance and in His power.

If those Galatians who received the Holy Spirit in power were tempted to go astray by that terrible danger of perfecting in the flesh what had been begun in the Spirit, how much more danger those Christians run who hardly ever know that they have received the Holy Spirit. How much more danger there is for those who, if they know it as a matter of belief, hardly ever think of the gift of the Holy Spirit, and hardly ever praise God for it!

Neglecting the Holy Spirit

But now look, in the second place, at the great danger of forgetting that we are to live by the Holy Spirit.

You may know what shunting is on a railway. A locomotive with its train may be traveling in a certain direction, and the points at some place may not be properly opened or closed, and it is shunted off to the right or to the left. And if this takes place, for instance, on a dark night, the train goes in the wrong direction, and the people might never know it until they have gone some distance.

Similarly, God gives Christians the Holy Spirit with this intention—that every day, all their lives, should be lived in the power of the Spirit. A man cannot live one hour of a godly life unless he lives by the power of the Holy Spirit. He may live a proper, consistent life, as people call it—an irreproachable life, a life of virtue and diligent service. But to live a life acceptable to God, in the enjoyment of God's salvation and God's love, to live and walk in the power of the new life—he cannot do it unless he is guided by the Holy Spirit every day and every hour.

But now pay attention to the danger. The Galatians received the Holy Spirit, but what was begun by the Spirit they tried to perfect in the flesh. How? They fell back again under Judaizing teachers who told them they must be circumcised. They began to seek their religion in external observances. And so Paul used that expression about those teachers who had them circumcised so *"that they may boast in your flesh"* (Galatians 6:13).

Sometimes I hear the expression "religious flesh" used. What is meant by this? It is simply an expression made to give utterance to these thoughts: my human nature and my human will and my human effort can be very active in religion. After being converted, and after receiving the Holy Spirit, I may begin in my own strength to try to serve God.

I may be very diligent and do a great deal, and yet all the time it is more the work of human flesh than of God's Spirit. What a solemn thought, that person can, without noticing, be shunted off from the line of the Holy Spirit onto the line of the flesh.

How solemn it is that man can be most diligent and make great sacrifices, and yet it is all in the power of the human will! Ah, the great question for us to ask of God in self-examination is that we may be shown whether our Christian lives are lived more in the power of the flesh than in the power of the Holy Spirit. A man may be a preacher and may work most diligently in his ministry; a man may be a Christian worker, and others may say of him that he makes great sacrifices, and yet you can sense there is something lacking. You sense that he is not a spiritual man; there is no spirituality about his life. How many Christians there are about whom no one would ever think of saying, "What a spiritual man he is!" Ah, here is the weakness of the church of Christ. It is all in this one word—*flesh*.

Now, the flesh may manifest itself in many ways. It may be manifested in fleshly wisdom. My mind may be most active about Christianity. I may preach or write or think or meditate, and delight in being occupied with things in God's Book and in God's kingdom. Yet the power of the Holy Spirit may be notably absent. I fear that if you take the preaching throughout the church of Christ and ask why there is so little converting power in the preaching of the Word, why there is so much work and often so little result for eternity, why the Word has so little power to build up believers in holiness and in consecration— the answer will be that the power of the Holy Spirit is absent. And why is this? There can be no other reason except that the flesh and human energy have taken the place that the Holy Spirit ought to have. This was true of the Galatians; it was true of the Corinthians. Paul said to them, *"I…could not speak to you as to spiritual people but as to carnal"* (1 Corinthians 3:1).

And you know how often in the course of his epistle he had to reprove and condemn them for strife and for divisions.

Lacking the Fruit of the Holy Spirit

A third thought is this: what are the proofs or indications that a church like the Galatians, or a Christian, is serving God in the power of the flesh—is perfecting in the flesh what was begun in the Spirit? The answer is very easy. Religious self-effort always ends in sinful flesh. What was the state of those Galatians? They were striving to be justified by the works of the law. And yet they were quarreling and in danger of devouring one another. Count the number of expressions that the apostle used to indicate their lack of love. You will find more than twelve: envy, jealousy, bitterness, strife, and all sorts of others. Read in the fourth and fifth chapters what he said about this. You see how they tried to serve God in their own strength, and they failed utterly. All this religious effort resulted in failure. The power of sin and the sinful flesh got the better of them. Their whole condition was one of the saddest that could be thought of.

This comes to us with unspeakable solemnity.

There is a complaint everywhere in the Christian church of the lack of a high standard of integrity and godliness, even among the professing members of

Christian churches. I remember a sermon that I heard preached on commercial morality. But let us not speak only of the commercial morality or immorality; let us go into the homes of Christians. Think of the life to which God has called His children, and that He enables them to live by the Holy Spirit. Think of how much there is of unlovingness, temper, sharpness, and bitterness. Think how often there is strife among the members of churches, and how much there is of envy, jealousy, oversensitivity, and pride. Then we are compelled to say, "Where are marks of the presence of the Spirit of the Lamb of God?" Lacking, sadly lacking!

Many people speak of these things as though they were the natural result of our feebleness and cannot be helped. Many people speak of these things as sins, yet have given up the hope of conquering them. Many people speak of these things in the church around them, and do not see the least prospect of ever having the things changed. There is no prospect until there is a radical change, until the church of God begins to see that every sin in the believer comes from the flesh—from a fleshly life amid our Christian activities, from a striving in self-effort to serve God. We will fail until we learn to make confession, and until we begin to see that we must somehow or other get God's Spirit in power back to His church. Where did the church begin at Pentecost? They began in the Spirit. But how the church of the next century went off into the flesh! They thought they could perfect the church in the flesh.

Do not let us think, because the Reformation restored the great doctrine of justification by faith, that the power of the Holy Spirit was then fully restored. If it is our belief that God is going to have mercy on His church in these last ages, it will be because the doctrine and the truth about the Holy Spirit will not only be studied, but sought after with a whole heart. It is not only because this truth will be sought after, but because ministers and congregations will be found bowing before God in deep abasement with one cry: "We have grieved God's Spirit. We have tried to be Christian churches with as little as possible of God's Spirit. We have not sought to be churches filled with the Holy Spirit."

All the feebleness in the church is owing to the refusal of the church to obey its God.

And why is this so? I know your answer. You say, "We are too feeble and too helpless, and we vow to obey, but somehow we fail."

Ah, yes, you fail because you do not accept the strength of God. God alone can work out His will in you. You cannot work out God's will, but His Holy Spirit can. Until the church and believers grasp this, cease trying by human effort to do God's will, and wait upon the Holy Spirit to come with all His omnipotent and enabling power, the church will never be what God wants her to be. It will never be what God is willing to make of her.

Yielding to the Holy Spirit

I come now to my last thought, the question, What is the way to restoration?

Beloved friend, the answer is simple and easy. If that train has been shunted off, there is nothing for it to do but to come back to the point at which it was led away. The Galatians had no other way of returning except to come back to where they had gone wrong. They had to come back from all religious effort in their own strength, and from seeking anything by their own work, and to yield themselves humbly to the Holy Spirit. There is no other way for us as individuals.

Is there any brother or sister whose heart is saying, "My life has little of the power of the Holy Spirit"?

I come to you with God's message—that you can have no idea of what your life would be in the power of the Holy Spirit. It is too high, too blessed, and too wonderful. But I bring you the message that just as truly as the everlasting Son of God came to this world and did His wonderful works, just as truly as on Calvary He died and brought about your redemption by His precious blood, so can the Holy Spirit come into your heart. With His divine power, He may sanctify you, enable you to do God's blessed will, and fill your heart with joy and strength.

We have forgotten, we have grieved, we have dishonored the Holy Spirit; and He has not been able to do His work. But I bring you the message that the Father in heaven loves to fill His children with His Holy Spirit. God longs to give each one individually, separately, the power of the Holy Spirit for daily life. The command comes to us individually, unitedly. God wants us as His children to arise and place our sins before Him, and to call on Him for mercy. Oh, are you so foolish? Are you perfecting in the flesh what was begun in the Spirit? Let us bow in shame and confess before God how our fleshly religion, our self-effort, and our self-confidence have been the cause of every failure.

I have often been asked by young Christians, "Why do I fail so? I did so solemnly vow with my whole heart, and did desire to serve God. Why have I failed?"

To such I always give this answer, "My dear friend, you are trying to do in your own strength what Christ alone can do in you."

And when they tell me, "I am sure I knew Christ alone could do it; I was not trusting in myself," my answer is, "You were trusting in yourself, or you could not have failed. If you had trusted Christ, He could not fail."

Oh, this perfecting in the flesh what was begun in the Spirit runs far deeper through us than we know. Let us ask God to show us that it is only when we are brought to utter shame and emptiness that we will be prepared to receive the blessing that comes from on high.

And so I come with these two questions. Are you living, beloved brother or sister—I ask it of every minister of the gospel—under the power of the Holy Spirit? Are you living as an anointed, Spirit-filled man or woman in your ministry and your life before God?

Oh, friends, our place is an awesome one. We have to show people what God will do for us, not in our words and teaching, but in our lives. God help us to do it!

I ask every member of Christ's church and every believer, Are you living a life under the power of the Holy Spirit day by day? Or are you attempting to live without His power? Remember, you cannot. Are you consecrated, given up to the Spirit to work in you and to live in you? Oh, come and confess every failure of temper, every failure of the tongue, however small. Confess every failure owing to the absence of the Holy Spirit and the presence of the power of self. Are you consecrated, are you given up to the Holy Spirit?

If your answer is no, then I come with a second question: Are you willing to be consecrated? Are you willing to give yourself up to the power of the Holy Spirit?

You well know that the human side of consecration will not help you. I may consecrate myself a hundred times with all the intensity of my being, and it will not help me. What will help me is this—that God from heaven accepts and seals the consecration.

And now, are you willing to give yourselves up to the Holy Spirit? You can do it now. A great deal may still be dark and dim, and beyond what we understand. You may feel nothing, but come. God alone can bring about the change. God alone, who gave us the Holy Spirit, can restore the Holy Spirit in power into our lives. God alone can strengthen us *"with might through His Spirit in the inner man"* (Ephesians 3:16). And to every waiting heart that will make the sacrifice, give up everything, and give time to cry and pray to God, the answer will come. The blessing is not far off. Our God delights in helping us. He will enable us to perfect, not in the flesh, but in the Spirit, what was begun in the Spirit.

8

THE KEEPING POWER OF GOD

Blessed be the God and Father of our Lord Jesus Christ, who…has begotten us again to a living hope through the resurrection of Jesus Christ from the dead, to an inheritance incorruptible…reserved in heaven for you, who are kept by the power of God through faith for salvation.
—1 Peter 1:3–5

Here we have two wonderful, blessed truths about the way a believer is kept unto salvation. One truth is *"kept by the power of God,"* and the other truth is *"kept…through faith."* We should look at the two sides—at God's side and His almighty power, offered to us to be our Keeper every moment of the day; and at the human side, on which we have nothing to do but in faith to let God do His keeping work. We are born again to an inheritance kept in heaven for us. We are kept here on earth by the power of God. We see there is a double keeping— the inheritance kept for me in heaven, and I on earth kept for the inheritance there.

Now, as to the first part of this keeping, there is no doubt and no question. God keeps the inheritance in heaven very wonderfully and perfectly, and it is waiting there safely. And the same God keeps me for the inheritance. This is what I want to examine in this chapter.

It is very foolish for a father to take great trouble to have an inheritance for his children, and to keep it for them, if he does not keep them for it. Think of a man spending all of his time and making every sacrifice to amass money, and as he gets his tens of thousands, you ask him why he sacrifices himself so. His answer is, "I want to leave my children a large inheritance, and I am keeping it for them." If you were then to hear that that man takes no trouble to educate his children, that he allows them to run wild on the streets and to go in paths of sin and ignorance and foolishness, what would you think of him? Would you not say, "Poor man! He is keeping an inheritance for his children, but he is not keeping or preparing his children for the inheritance"? And there are so many Christians who think, "My God is keeping the inheritance for me," but they cannot believe, "My God is keeping me for that inheritance." The same power, the same love, the same God is doing the double work.

Now, I want to write about a work God does upon us—keeping us for the inheritance. I have already said that we have two very simple truths: the one, the divine side, is that we are *"kept by the power of God"*; the other, the human side, is that we are *"kept…through faith."*

Kept by the Power of God

Look at the divine side: Christians are *"kept by the power of God."*

• Keeping Includes All

Think, first of all, that this keeping is all-inclusive. What is kept? You are kept. How much of you? The whole being. Does God keep one part of you and not another? No. Some people have an idea that this is a sort of vague, general keeping, and that God will keep them in such a way that when they die they will get to heaven. But they do not apply the word *"kept"* to everything in their beings and natures. And yet this is what God wants.

Suppose I have a watch and that this watch had been borrowed from a friend. Suppose the friend said to me, "When you go to Europe, I will let you take it with you, but make sure you keep it safely and bring it back."

Suppose I damaged the watch—the hands are broken, the face is defaced, and some of the wheels and springs are spoiled—and took it back to my friend in that condition. He would say, "Ah, but I gave you that watch on the condition that you would keep it."

"Have I not kept it? Here is the watch."

"But I did not want you to keep it in that general way, so that you would bring me back only the shell of the watch, or the remains. I expected you to keep every part of it."

Similarly, God does not want to keep us in this general way, so that at the last, somehow or other, we will be saved as by fire, and just get into heaven. But the keeping power and the love of God applies to every part of our beings.

Some people think God will keep them in spiritual things, but not in temporal things. The latter, they say, lies outside of His realm. Now, God sends you to work in the world, but He did not say, "I must now leave you to go and earn your own money, and to get your livelihood for yourself." He knows you are not able to keep yourself. But God says, "My child, there is no work you are to do, and no business in which you are engaged, and not a cent you are to spend, but I, your Father, will take that up into My keeping." God not only cares for the spiritual, but also for the temporal. The greater part of many people's lives must be spent, sometimes eight or nine or ten hours a day, amid the temptations and distractions of business. But God will care for you there. The keeping of God includes all.

Other people think, "Ah, in time of trial God keeps me. But in times of prosperity I do not need His keeping; then I forget Him and let Him go." Others, again, think the very opposite. They think, "In time of prosperity, when things are smooth and quiet, I am able to cling to God. But when heavy trials come, somehow or other my will rebels, and God does not keep me then."

Now, I bring you the message that in prosperity as in adversity, in the sunshine as in the dark, your God is ready to keep you all the time.

Then again, others think of this keeping in this way: "God will keep me from doing very great wickedness, but there are small sins I cannot expect God to keep me from. There is the sin of a bad temper. I cannot expect God to conquer that."

When you hear of some man who has been tempted and gone astray or fallen into drunkenness or murder, you thank God for His keeping power.

"I might have done the same as that man," you say, "if God had not kept me." And you believe He kept you from drunkenness and murder.

And why do you not believe that God can keep you from outbreaks of temper? You thought that this was of less importance. You did not remember that the great commandment of the New Testament is, *"Love one another; as I have loved you"* (John 13:34). And when your temper and hasty judgment and sharp words came out, you sinned against the highest law—the law of God's love. And yet you say, "God does not keep me from that." You perhaps say, "He can; but there is something in me that cannot attain it, and that God does not take away."

I want to ask you, Can believers live a holier life than is generally lived? Can believers experience the keeping power of God all day, to keep them from sin? Can believers be kept in fellowship with God? And I bring you a message from the Word of God, in these words: *"Kept by the power of God."* There is no qualifying clause to them. The meaning is this: if you will entrust yourself entirely and absolutely to the omnipotence of God, He will delight in keeping you.

Some people think that they can never reach the point at which every word of their mouths would be to the glory of God. But it is what God wants of them; it is what God expects of them. God is willing to set a watchman at the door of their mouths. (See Psalm 141:3.) If God will do that, can He not keep their tongues and their lips? He can. This is what God is going to do for those who trust Him. God's keeping is all-inclusive. Let everyone who desires to live a holy life think about all his needs, his weaknesses, his shortcomings, and his sins, and say deliberately,

"Is there any sin that my God cannot keep me from?" And the heart will have to answer, "No, God can keep me from every sin."

✦ Keeping Requires Power

Second, if you want to understand this keeping, remember that it is not only an all-inclusive keeping, but also an almighty keeping.

I want to get this truth burned into my soul. I want to worship God until my whole heart is filled with the thought of His omnipotence. God is almighty, and the almighty God offers Himself to work in my heart—to do the work of keeping me. I want to get linked with omnipotence, or rather, linked to the omnipotent One—the living God—and to have my place in the hollow of His hand. You read the Psalms, and you think of the wonderful thoughts in many of the expressions that David used. For instance, he spoke about our God being our *"fortress"* (Psalm 18:2), our *"refuge"* (Psalm 28:8), our *"strong tower"* (Psalm 61:3), our *"strength"* (Psalm 18:1), and our *"salvation"* (Psalm 27:1). David had wonderful views of how the everlasting God is Himself the hiding place of the believing soul. David had a beautiful understanding of how God takes the believer and keeps him in the very hollow of His hand—in the secret of His pavilion (see Psalm 27:5)—under the shadow of His wings (see Psalm 17:8), under His very feathers (see Psalm 91:4). David lived there. And we, who are the children of Pentecost, who have known Christ, His blood, and the Holy Spirit sent down from heaven, why do we know so little of what it is to walk step by step with the almighty God as our Keeper?

Have you ever thought that, in every action of grace in your heart, you have the whole omnipotence of God engaged to bless you? When I come to a man and he gives me a gift of money, I get it and go away with it. He has given me something of his. He keeps the rest for himself. But it is not this way with the power of God. God can part with nothing of His own power, and therefore I can experience the power and goodness of God only so far as I am in contact and fellowship with Him. And when I come into contact and fellowship with Him, I come into contact and fellowship with the whole omnipotence of God. I have the omnipotence of God to help me every day.

Suppose that a son has a very rich father, and as the former is about to commence business the father says, "You can have as much money as you want for your undertaking." All the father has is at the disposal of the son. This is the way with God, your almighty God. You can hardly take it in; you feel like such a little worm. His omnipotence is needed to keep a little worm! Yes, His omnipotence is needed to keep every little worm that lives in the dust, and also to keep the universe. Therefore, His omnipotence is much more needed in keeping your soul and mine from the power of sin.

Oh, if you want to grow in grace, learn to begin here. In all your judgings and meditations and thoughts and deeds and questions and studies and prayers, learn to be kept by your almighty God. What is the almighty God not going to do for the child who trusts Him? The Bible says He will do *above all that we ask or think* (Ephesians 3:20). It is omnipotence you must learn to know and trust. Then you will live as a Christian ought to live. How little we have learned to study God, and to understand that a godly life is a life full of God. It is a life that loves God and waits on Him, trusts Him, and allows Him to bless it! We cannot do the will of God except by the power of God. God gives us the first experience of His power to prepare us to desire more, and to come and claim all that He can do. God helps us to trust Him every day.

✦ *Keeping Is Continuous*

Another thought is that this keeping is not only all-inclusive and omnipotent, but also continuous and unbroken.

People sometimes say, "For a week or a month God has kept me very wonderfully. I have lived in the light of His countenance, and I can say what joy I have had in fellowship with Him. He has blessed me in my work for others. He has given me souls, and at times I felt as if I were carried heavenward on eagles' wings. But it did not continue. It was too good; it could not last." And some say, "It was necessary that I should fall to keep me humble." And others say, "I know it was my own fault, but somehow you cannot always live up in the heights."

Oh, beloved, why is it? Can there be any reason why the keeping of God should not be continuous and unbroken? Just think; all life is in unbroken continuity. If my life were stopped for half an hour, I would be dead, and my life would be gone. Life is a continuous thing, and the life of God is the life of His church. The life of God is His almighty power working in us. And God comes to us as the almighty One, and without any condition He offers to be my Keeper. His keeping means that day by day, moment by moment, God is going to keep us.

If I were to ask you the question, "Do you think God is able to keep you one day from actual transgression?" you would answer, "I not only know He is able to do it, but I think He has done it. There have been days in which He has kept my heart in His holy presence. There have also been days when, though I have always had a sinful nature within me, He has kept me from conscious, actual transgression."

Now, if He can do that for an hour or a day, why not for two days? Oh, let us make God's omnipotence as revealed in His Word the measure of our expectations. Has God not said in His Word, *"I, the Lord, keep it, I water it every moment"* (Isaiah 27:3)? What can this mean? Does *"every moment"* mean every moment? Did God promise of that vineyard that every moment He would water it so that the heat of the sun and the scorching wind might never dry it up? Yes.

Will our God, in His tenderhearted love toward us, not keep us every moment when He has promised to do so? Oh, if we once got hold of the thought that our entire spiritual lives are to be God's doing! *"It is God who works in you both to will and to do for His good*